𝔚alking 𝔚ith the 𝔚ichita ℘ioneers

𝔄 𝔊uidebook to ℌighland ℭemetery

1005 N. Hillside
Wichita, Kansas

Compiled By:
Barb Myers

Forward by Dr. Jay Price

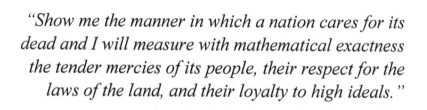

"Show me the manner in which a nation cares for its dead and I will measure with mathematical exactness the tender mercies of its people, their respect for the laws of the land, and their loyalty to high ideals."

Sir William Ewart Gladstone (December 29, 1809 – May 19, 1898)

"Successful Cemetery Advertising"; The American Cemetery, March 1938

DEDICATION:

To my parents, who made every day of my research possible, and all of my dreams come true.

To Kyra, the brightest light on my darkest days.

And to Carl, who kept on pushing me, even after he was gone.

Forward

A Local History Book in Stone

Dr. Jay Price

Since the 1870s, Highland Cemetery has been a window into Wichita's story. Her early founders are buried here as are their families. The names on the gravestones such as Greiffenstein, Munger, Mead, Meagher, English, Steele, Lawrence, Snitzler, Sowers, and Harris read like a "who's who" of early Wichita. Whatever their issues and challenges in life, they have come to rest here, side by side, overlooking the city they helped establish. As the years passed, Highland became the final home of the city's residents both great and small. Mayors and political leaders rest near infants and children.

Yet, the divisions, identities, and distinctions of these earlier generations do remain, now preserved forever in the stone landscape at Highland. Military service appears in the markers of veterans. Other stones bear the symbols of the Freemasons, Odd Fellows, and Woodmen of the World. Some individuals and families sought to show their influence through ornate monuments and sculptures. Others preferred more humble memorials. Groupings of graves reveal how family ties connected individuals.

Birth and death dates tell their own stories. Some birth dates go back to the 1700s, reminding us that the pioneers of Wichita were not that far removed from the founding years of the nation as a whole. The shorter lifespans remind us how often diseases and accidents claimed even the very young in those early times.

Location can reveal its own lessons. Highland is next to the cemetery of Congregation Emanu-El, the resting place of Wichita's reform Jewish community. Early Jewish Wichitans with names such as Wallenstein and Cohn rest next to the Gentile families with whom they worked, served, and struggled. Across the street is Maple Grove, developed in the 1880s the elegant Victorian cemetery that symbolized Wichita's transformation from a small town on the frontier into a modern metropolis.

Cemeteries can also reveal divisions and issues of race and discrimination. At Highland, the burial of African Americans was connected to attitudes of race and class. There are reasons why the graves of this city's African American residents are clustered in certain areas and not others.

Cemeteries, therefore, provide useful insights into a location's story, its people, and its issues. Moreover, like textbooks, they can be forgotten and overlooked. Books and cemeteries can be neglected and lost unless individuals step forward to care and preserve them. That is why this effort on the part of the Friends of the Wichita Pioneers is so significant. They have taken the effort to document the graves, clear brush, set up headstones, give tours, and publish guides like this one. Therefore, as you walk among the stones at Highland, let this book be an introduction to the neighbors that you never knew you had.

ACKNOWLEDGEMENTS:

A very sincere thank you to everyone who helped research or work on Highland with me: Mom, Dad and Scott; Kyra; Carl; Bill Pennington; Nancy and Steve Perry; Dr. Jay Price; Jim Mason; Mike Maxton; Shannon Reed; Rhenee Swink; Kyle Palmer; Dalton Sanders; Janiece and Curtis Dixon; Kim and Ralph Hebert; Joe Baughman; Charles Myers; Becky Hunter; Nicole Conard; Val Ellington; Dr. James Mershon Mary Lou Rivers; Gary Steed; Lynn Rogers; Beccy Tanner; David Stuart; Mike Gerik; Vince Marshall; Bev Henline; Carol Peterson; Jack Kellogg; Pat O'Connor; Ken Spurgeon; John Rodda; William Sloane; Todd Phifer of Cochran Mortuary; Paul Oberg; The City of Wichita Park Department; Wichita City Council; Gary Huffman of First Presbyterian Church; Katie Potts and St. John's Episcopal Church; Eric Cale and Jami Frazier Tracy of Wichita Sedgwick County Historical Museum; Julia Langel of the Midwest Genealogical Historical Society; Mary Nelson of WSU Special Collections; Keith Wondra of Old Cowtown Museum; Mark McCormick of The Kansas African American Museum; Kansas State Historical Society; Kansas University Special Collections; Hal Ottaway; Hal George of Maple Grove Cemetery; Jim Grawe of KPTS; my vast, unpaid research team on Facebook; soooooo many donors and volunteers; and of course the families of those who are buried at Highland, without whom there would be no stories left to tell.

All dates of death and burial places are verified by KsGenWeb.org, a website that is maintained by Bill Pennington; on BillionGraves; and on FindAGrave, a site that links to Ancestry.com. The writer is indebted to all of these sites and their contributors. Any incorrect information or omissions are solely mine, and no reflection on the contributors to these pages.

Walking with the Wichita Pioneers-
A Guidebook to Highland Cemetery

Table of Contents:

Use your web enabled smartphone's scanner app
to open the above QR code. This will take you to the City of Wichita's
Park and Recreation website.

This website gives the user access to Highland Cemetery's plot records;
FindaGrave records; &
Friends of the Wichita Pioneers Facebook page.

Maps of the separate sections begin on page 152.

AUTHOR'S INTRODUCTION.

Name one thing we all have in common. Go ahead, I'll wait....

Yes, we all die eventually. And what did all people in Wichita have in common from 1868-1888? They were all buried at Highland Cemetery. (ok, except for those occasional burials by the river.)

Because death is such a taboo topic, I get asked a lot "WHY do you want to do this?" So- let me tell you....

In 2014, I was taking a Kansas history class at Wichita State University. I needed to research Wichita history, and in doing so, I noticed how many of the people I was researching were buried at Highland. I had no idea the history of the cemetery, only that there were many interesting people buried there. So, step one was my taking the Kansas history class and step two was the specific research of the history Wichita. The problem was: There were very few records, and it appeared that little had ever been written about the cemetery.

Then came the work.... Step three was when I decided to share what I had found. So that is when I started giving historical tours of the cemetery and talks in the community. We discuss not only the history of Highland, and of Wichita, but also cemetery etiquette and burial customs. As I would like to be an educator, it is important to me that I can teach what I have learned to others. After that, I started one Facebook page, Wichita History From My Perspective. Then another, called Friends of the Wichita Pioneers, just for study of the cemetery.

The next step of the process started while I was giving tours. Participants asked if there was anything we could do to fix the stones that were in such bad shape. So, I started looking at what needed to be done. Since the city of Wichita owns the cemetery, we would have to get permission to make any repairs or changes to it. So, in 2017, I filed for non-profit status, which was for the purpose of saving the city tax money by taking care of the cemetery without taking money from the park department's budget. The only funds we would have access to would be by donations or grants. At that point we entered into a Memorandum of Understanding with the City, which would allow us to preserve the cemetery. The only caveat is that we must have permission from the families. We are historians! We can make this happen!

The final step then, is this book. The research I have done is for a thesis project for my graduate studies. This book is the abbreviated version of that research.

This is what I found in my research.

Why ancestry matters:

Wichita was founded by immigrants and homesteaders from all over the world. Therefore, not surprisingly, Highland has burials from Germany, Ireland, Scotland, England, Sweden, Greece, Lebanon, Mexico, and Viet Nam.

Why religion matters:

People from many religions such as Catholic, Episcopal, Presbyterian, Methodist, Baptist—well, basically all Protestants--and of course Jews are buried at Highland. Even Pagans, Gypsies and the Salvation Army are represented.

Many different cultures are represented at Highland, and every one of their cultural beliefs fascinate me. For example, Pagans and Native Americans have a reliance upon animal spirit guides. I find that most interesting because it happens to me all the time at Highland. I have been guided to grave markers by a fox, a dog, crows, hawks, rabbits, and even a skink. Animals have insight that we do not. I follow them whenever possible, because for me, they are always right.

Why social class matters:

Based on what I already knew about the families (for instance, city founders and business leaders,) I noticed an obvious disparity in financial class. Literally, at the top of the hill, (elevation 1,358 feet) at the intersection of blocks one, two, three and four seemed to be mainly for the burials of the affluent; the outer areas are for the mainly middle class; and block four trends toward the lower class.

Why race matters:

Probably the most surprising thing I found out about Highland was the division NOT of culture, but of race. [1] One thing I wanted to find out was "why?" What laws were there in Wichita and in Kansas that required segregation? (Were there actual de jure laws that enabled the cemetery to be segregated? Or were there just de facto 'Jim Crow' laws, that allowed it to happen by circumstance?)

One thing I also looked at was the neighborhood. Highland is in a low income, mostly African American neighborhood. So, would a white neighborhood have been able to "keep out" blacks by methods such as covenants? This might have been a possibility, until 1948, when the Beatty v. Kurtz case made it illegal for covenants to disallow blacks from a neighborhood. And black movement was INTO that area, not out. So no, the neighborhood Highland is in did not make a difference in who was buried there. Or, was it by contractual design? No, I have found no contracts that would be proof of that. So, the conclusion I came to is that the racial divide at Highland had to have been made by Highland's own

---

[1] See Table 1.

14

management, (which I will explain later,) but was persisted by personal choice. Families choose to be buried by family members, and that is human nature. Luckily, in 1964 it also became law that anyone could have been buried anywhere they wanted to be. A breakdown of burials by race is given in Table 1.

The point is this: Different people refer to death differently. African Americans call it home-going. Native Americans and Pagans call it returning to Mother Earth. Jews refer to burial as 'ashes to ashes'. Muslims must be buried within the next day, and other religions require a waiting period of three days. While Catholics have a large mass and might even fast, Methodists often have large get-togethers with food. Some services are somber affairs, and some play Dixieland music. Some people have huge markers, others don't want one at all. But one thing is always the same: We all die, and we all deserve a kind and respectful burial, in a cemetery plot of our own choosing. This is the story of one such cemetery — the oldest cemetery in Wichita: Highland Cemetery.

CHAPTER ONE:

In the Beginning...

In 1857, before Wichita even existed, Ewing Moxley and Edmund Mosely operated a trading post at what is now 61st and Seneca. Edmund Mosely came here with his family, and after an indian raid they left for a quieter life. However, he was drawn back to Comanche County, where he died in an Osage indian raid. He is buried by the river there. Ewing Moxley left the area by the beginning of the Civil War and led a much less quiet life than he had in Sedgwick County area. He was drowned in 1864 crossing the Kansas River in Lawrence, while stealing contraband stock.[2]

C. C. Arnold and Robert Durackin[3] settled in the area around the same time, and a few years later (1860?) John Ross and his family moved in north of what is now Sedgwick County. Arnold and Durackin moved on to Chelsea. John was killed and found "in pieces" by his paid help. (Of course, in James R. Mead's opinion, the help may have actually killed him.)[4] His family moved soon after his murder, and his cabin was left empty. Years later, Mead stayed in that same cabin while hunting buffalo on the prairie. The land at 77th and 103rd (Maize) was later known as Old Park City, and then the Jewett Farm.[5]

After that, the area we call Wichita attracted very few white settlers for several years. That is, until the Osage Treaties, and Jesse Chisholm, William Greiffenstein, and James R. Mead and the Wichita Town Company became interested in the area once again.

---

[2] Bear Grease, Builders and Bandits; Andreas, 1384; Hunting and Trading on the Great Plains, page 140.
[3] Durackin is spelled a number of ways. We use the spelling from Chapman's book here.
[4] Wichita the Early Years, page 6; Hunting and Trading, page 142.
[5] Cutler, Part 1; Park City thesis, page 26; Chapman, p. 196-97.

The Moxley/Mosely Trading Post marker.

It is located in the area of 61st and Seneca on personal property.

The 1865 Osage Treaty marker is located on the NW corner of

W 61st Street N & N Seneca Street. Placed 1925.

CHAPTER TWO:

The Life and Times of Highland Cemetery, Part I

Henry Smith was born in Leicestershire, England on Sept 24, 1837. He immigrated to Utica, NY in 1849 with his father Joshua, step mother Mary and several of his siblings. In 1854-55 the family moved to Lawrence, Kansas, where Henry farmed until 1868.

Siblings (Mother: Elizabeth Chambers Smith, died of typhus 1841.)

Rebecca Smith. - Stayed in England.

Emma Smith. - Died young, in England.

*John Smith – (1832-1915.) Served in the 11th Regiment in the US Cavalry. Came to Kansas with the family and moved on to Wabaunsee as a member of the Beecher Bible and Rifle Colony. He was a conductor in the Underground Railroad. John stayed in Wabaunsee and is buried there.[6]

Step-siblings (Mother: Mary Cook Smith):

*William Smith (1843-1908.) First wife, Mary Peck.

Buried at Galena with his second wife and their family.

*Mary Mossman (1845-1929.) Married to John. 4-323-4.

*Emma Goodyear (1853-1931.) Married to Charles. 4-289-9.[7]

Frederick T Smith: Born in Lawrence, KS. (1854-1911). 4-322-8.[8]

---

[6] FindaGrave entry for John Smith, accessed July 3, 2018. The entry says John came to America at age 16 with his father, step mother, Henry, and two other small children.

[7] Emma would have been born in Lawrence, depending on when they actually came to America. Records differ.

[8] Joshua Smith's probate file is at MHGS, file #1522. His executor, son Fred T. Smith

(* Born in England and came to America.)

In 1868, Henry and his brother William moved to Wichita to operate a sawmill on the Little Arkansas, for the growing town.[9] Henry pre-empted a quarter section after April 10, 1869, when Osage Land became available by law.

Henry claimed that fifteen people were already buried on the hill when he first settled there. .[10] So, in 1870 he deeded land which he had intended to farm, to the city for use as the city's cemetery.

In July 21, 1870 Wichita became an incorporated city of the third class.

On April 4, 1871, Henry paid \$1.25 an acre for a 160-acre section. That \$200.00 section is on the northeast corner of 9th and Hillside.

1871 Henry Smith married Hattie Royal, John T. Royal's sister. They had one son, Arthur.

The Wichita Cemetery Company incorporated on February 3, 1872. Board members were mostly family: Henry Smith, Joshua Smith, William Smith, John Mossman, and John T. Royal, but also J. McCulloch and Fred A. Sowers. [11] The County has owned the area north of the cemetery since 1872.[12]

---

lists what he thought his family members and their ages were in 1893.

[9] Wichita Eagle, August 10, 1995; Chapman, 1888, page 338.

[10] Ibid.

[11] Wichita Daily Eagle, Dec 6, 1908; Sagacity magazine, Vol 3, No 2, Spring 1998, Eric Cale; See plats filed with Sedgwick County

[12] Wichita Sunday Eagle, Sunday, March 15, 1964

On March 22, 1872, the Wichita Cemetery Company platted Highland Cemetery. [13]

Land Grant.

---

[13] Wichita Eagle, December 6, 1908.

Henry received his land grant on May 1, 1873 after making the required improvement to the land. His homestead became known as 2704 E. Frisco (now 9th Street.) According to Henry's grandson Elmer Smith, Henry began to sell plots for $15 to $20 per lot in the Spring of 1870.[14]

MAP of HIGHLAND CEMETERY

CEM-4-4

1872 Plat: Each block has its own numbering system.

Graves in each plot are laid out like "ice cube trays," where number 1 would be the SE corner and 7 would be the NW corner. In most cases feet face the east, and a headstone would be on the west end. But that is certainly not always the case. At Highland, you will find the headstone at the east as often as at the west end of a grave.

---

[14] Sunday Growler, 1887; Wichita Eagle, August 10, 1995

(NORTH)

7	6
8	5
9	4
10	3
11	2
12	1

(Potter's Field is numbered differently. See page 162.)

A person could buy single, quarter, half or whole plots. In some cases, burials were stacked, but not more than two high. Vaults were not required until the 1900s, so the whole area could be used, and an actual burial could be anywhere within the block. Whole plots are 20' x 15'. Single plots are 3.33' x 7.5'

William, step brother of Henry Smith, was the Marshal in 1873 and the Sheriff from 1874-75. He left in 1878 for the new town of Galena. William's first wife Mary is buried at Highland with the Smith family.

July 20, 1874 Henry's first wife Hattie Smith died. She was married to Henry in 1871, and they had one child, Arthur. Hattie Smith is in 4-287.

Hattie Smith's grave marker.

July 24, 1875 Henry Smith married Sarah Lewis Skinner. They had six children:

Hattie Carr: 1876-1938. Children: Blanche, Hazel and Earl.

    She and her family are located in 1-61.

Grace Rhodes: 1878-1950. No children.

    She and her husband are located in 4-77.

Harry Smith: No children.

    He and his wife are located in 4-77.

Florence Cave: 1886-1938. Children: Helen and Robert.

    Their family is located in 4-287.

Ina Francis Bobbitt Cave: 1888-1971. She had two children.

    She is located in 4-287.

    (After Florence died in 1938, Ina married her widower, Ralph E. Cave. He died in 1948. They are both buried near him.)

Charles L.: 1890-1911?? Charles had a son named Elmer.[15]

Courtesy of Elmer Smith

In 1870, Henry Smith deeded part of his farmland to the city of Wichita for use as Highland Cemetery.

---

[15] Wichita Eagle, August 10, 1995.

1883 The Wichita Cemetery Association was one of four organizations mentioned in William Cutler's History of the State of Kansas, Sedgwick County.[16]

1885 "Beautifying the Abode of the Dead" article, describing how the cemetery looked in 1885, and some changes being made by the Powell, Dill, Richey and Daisy families at the time. Those changes were said to include fences, sidewalks and walls. However, those do not remain, so there is no evidence that they were ever completed.[17]

1885 Because Jews and Gentiles must be buried separately, according to Jewish custom, the Temple Emanuel bought land at Highland for $600.00, for their own cemetery.[18] The fence that is around that part of the cemetery was put in place by the Congregation.

[16] History of the State of Kansas, William Cutler, published 1883 by A. T. Andreas, Chicago, ILL. End of Section 5.
[17] Wichita Daily Eagle, August 22, 1885.
[18] Wichita Beacon, November 9, 1885.

1886 Henry Smith's home at 2704 E. Frisco was completed, at a cost of $3,200.00.[19]   The cemetery would be to the east, or to the right of the house in these pictures.

Image courtesy of the family of Henry Smith, 2017. Date unknown.

(Google Maps.)

_____

[19] Chapman, 1888; p. 778-79.

Frisco Street is now called 9th. The location of his former home is now known as Liberty Way Apartment Community.

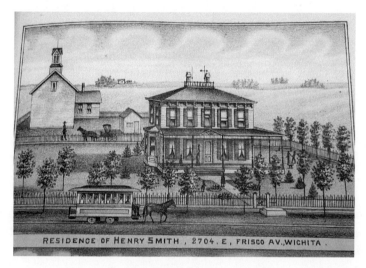

RESIDENCE OF HENRY SMITH, 2704. E, FRISCO AV.,WICHITA.

Picture from Chapman's 1888 Sedgwick County History, page 338-39.

April 18, 1886 "Our Lonely Cemetery" letter to the editor in the Daily Eagle. The letter which was a criticism of the current state of the cemetery, was signed by K.

1887 Martin S. Rochelle is given the job of sexton of Highland by the Wichita Cemetery Company. (John T. Royal was the manager at the time.)[20]

Rochelle is buried at Maple Grove Cemetery.

---

[20] Wichita Eagle, April 14, 1887; Ibid, April 26, 1887.

December 1887 *Sunday Growler* article published about the current ownership of Highland. It is the first mention of the fifteen people which were buried on the hill that was owned by Henry Smith, when he received the land.[21]

1888 Maple Grove cemetery was founded by A. A. Hyde and Martin L. Garver of Grace Presbyterian Church, the same year that Hyde founded the Yucca Soap Co.

1888 Henry Smith was the Township treasurer, road supervisor and a school trustee. [22]

August 17, 1889 Wichita Cemetery Company conveyed the deed for Highland to Henry Smith by quit claim, for all of the land except the Jewish Cemetery.

Nov 30, 1893 Family patriarch Joshua Smith died. He is located in 4-288 next to his second wife, Mary.

[21] Sunday Growler, December 11, 1887.
[22] Chapman, 1888. Page 338-39.

Sept. 1898 "Ought to Be Improved" letter to the Editor, Marshall Murdock, about the current state of Highland Cemetery. From the Ladies' Highland Cemetery Improvement Association. This included Mrs. Henry Schnitzler, Mrs. L. C. Hickman, Mrs. W. C. Copeland, Mrs. G. Gehring, Mrs. J. P. Stout, Mrs. A. L. Park, and Mrs. Corwin.[23]

Sept. 1898 "Shafts of Marble" editorial response, by Marshall Murdock. He talked about the beauty of the cemetery. Interestingly, his letter also mentions the street car line.[24]

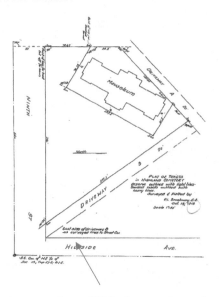

(This unfiled plat map from 1915 shows where the driveway formerly ran- in front of the mausoleum, from the corner of 9th and Hillside west of the GAR section of the cemetery. The streetcar picked up at the corner. There was also a carriage road that went around the mausoleum.)

In 1899, Henry sold the property to the Principals of Maple Grove, who renamed the ownership company the "Highland Cemetery Association."

[23] Wichita Daily Eagle, September 20, 1898
[24] Ibid, September 21, 1898.

There were several subsequent advertisements in *The Wichita Beacon* and *Wichita Eagle*, showing Henry Smith as "Manager".[25] However, in 1882 a Supreme Court Case had ruled "it is offensive to operate a tax-exempt cemetery for profit," which would become a problem for Maple Grove's ownership of Highland.[26]

HIGHLAND CEMETERY NOTICE:

> To whom it may concern: On and after this date all business connected with the above-named cemetery will be in my charge. I will make deeds for lots and improve the same; dig graves and any other work connected with the cemetery. Call upon or telephone Henry Smith, manager.
>
> Wichita Feb. 13, 1899

January 1900 "Home of the Dead" article published. Highland Cemetery Improvement Association held a fund raiser with Judge T. B. Wall as the lecturer on Ulysses Grant.[27]

In 1901 Highland Cemetery Association's "permanent" office was located in the City building.[28]

October 1902 Noted as being the third year of work being done by the Highland Cemetery Association.[29]

November 1, 1903 Meeting of Highland Cemetery Association held.

---

[25] Wichita Beacon, February 16, 1899; Sagacity, Vol 3, No. 2, Spring 1998
[26] Mitford, page 84-85.
[27] Wichita Daily Eagle, January 24, 1900
[28] Ibid, June 28, 1901
[29] Ibid, October 5, 1902.

December 1903 Members of the Cemetery Association will raise a "care fund" for Highland's upkeep.[30]

May 1904 Ladies of the Highland Cemetery Association to hold a benefit reception at the home of Mrs. Marsh.[31]

July 1907 After complaints about the neglect at Highland, A.A. Hyde made a rebuttal in regard to the Highland Cemetery Improvement Company's management of Highland. In his letter, he also discusses improvements made by them, such as the addition of a street car building. He was apparently also a big fan of Mrs. Martha Ferguson, who had been the caretaker of the records of Highland. Mrs. Ferguson is located in 1-246.[32] (Not surprisingly, A. A. Hyde is buried at Maple Grove.)

May 1908 New Lot owner trustees – John Davidson, Jr; Alf C. Goodin; Finlay Ross; Farley A. Gackenbach; and Martha Ferguson.[33]

Gill Mortuary has been recreated at Cowtown. This is what a mourning room would have looked like in the Victorian era.

---

[30] Wichita Daily Eagle, December 16, 1903
[31] Ibid, May 14, 1904.
[32] ibid, July 31, 1907
[33] Ibid, May 23, 1908

May 26, 1908 Henry Smith died. He had been in an accident a month before. He is located in 4-287-9 next to both of his wives:

Hattie (4-287-10) and Sarah (4-287-8.)[34]

[34] Wichita Beacon, May 27, 1908.

CHAPTER THREE:

The Life and Times of Highland Cemetery, Part II

The cemetery was operated by Maple Grove until 1908. But because of the question of legality of a for-profit company owning a municipal cemetery, the principals of Maple Grove were forced to give it back to the lot owners.

1908 Henry's brother William Smith died. He is buried in Galena, KS, the next city he helped found.

July 1908 Demand possession made by lot owners (The Wichita Cemetery Co) represented by John Davidson, Jr; Alf C. Goodin; Martha Ferguson; Finlay Ross; and Farley A. Gackenbach.[35] On December 6, 1908, $2,250.00 is then turned over to the Lot Owner Trustees John Davidson, Jr; Finlay Ross; Alf C. Goodin; Farley A Gackenbach; and Martha Ferguson. The article also lists the first officers, in 1872.[36]

June 21, 1910 Hillside Street paved. Taxes were assessed to both Maple Grove and Highland. But Highland never paid their portion, a decision which would lead to future legal action.[37]

1911 Frederick T. Smith, youngest brother of Henry, died in Wichita. He was the "second white child" born in Lawrence, KS, in 1854. Fred is located with his daughter Dorothy in 4-322. His wife and other children are buried in Pawhuska, Oklahoma (formerly, Indian Territory.)

---

[35] Wichita Eagle Article, July 1908.
[36] Ibid, December 6, 1908.
[37] Wichita Beacon article, June 21, 1910

1911 Wichita Mausoleum at Highland Cemetery platted.

June 15, 1911 John T. Royal died. He had been the manager of the cemetery since the early 1880s and was Henry's brother in law. He moved to Wichita in 1871 and lived at 2520 E. 9th. John and his family are located in 4-286-8, next to the family of Henry Smith. [38]

June 1913 "To Build Mammoth Sepulchre" article. Mausoleum work began, with George A. Saxton of the American Cemetery Co in the lead. The mausoleum was finished in 1916 and would accommodate over 300 bodies. George Saxton oversaw this project, and later built the Old Mission Mausoleum.[39]

August 31, 1915 The Wichita Mausoleum Association incorporated. The land was deeded from the Wichita Cemetery Company to the Wichita Mausoleum Association on October 18, 1915. However, there was a filing error, and in 1965 when the mausoleum's incorporation expired, the City was shown as owner of the land.

[38] Wichita Beacon, June 16, 1911.
[39] Ibid, June 12, 1913; Wichita Eagle June 13, 1913; October 26, 1919; May 2, 2004

August 6, 1916 Wichita Mausoleum at Highland Cemetery finished. The *Wichita Eagle's* article "Tomb is Beautiful Structure."

1920 Article saying the Highland Cemetery Improvement Association wants a second mausoleum, which ultimately did not happen. Mrs. T. H Huffman, president of the Improvement Association is also now buried at Highland, in 1-202.

December 19, 1920 *Wichita Eagle* article about one of the first burials, in 1871.[40]

August 1921 Notice of the Annual Meeting of the Wichita Cemetery Company. John Davidson, Jr. President; Alf C. Goodin, Secretary; and Farley A. Gackenbach, Treasurer did not run for office again, so elections were held. Officers elected were Henry Schnitzler, Sr, President and R. W. Park, Secretary.[41]

1921 New officers elected-Wichita Cemetery Company. Lot owners Henry Schnitzler, Sr, President and R.W. Park, Secretary/Treasurer were elected.

August 1922 Annual Lot Owners' Meeting notice, for September 13, 1922. Henry Schnitzler, Sr. President; R. W. Park secretary.[42]

September 1922 *Beacon* article about the first five cemeteries: Highland, Maple Grove, Calvary, White Chapel and Old Mission. The article also mentions the Jewish Cemetery at Highland.[43]

---

[40] Wichita Eagle, Dec 19, 1920; page B-9
[41] Ibid, August 9, 1921.
[42] Wichita Beacon, August 9, 1922.
[43] Ibid, Sept. 17, 1922

Sept. 27, 1924 Block 5 plat filed by Henry Schnitzler, Sr. and R. W. Park. The plat was approved by the City Council on July 10, 1925.

1926 Replat of block 2R filed.

August 7, 1929 Sarah E. Lewis-Skinner-Smith died. She was Henry's second wife and is located next to him, in 4-287-8.

1935 John Davidson, Jr. is reported as being the president of the lot owner's association.

John Davidson, Jr. is located with the Davidson family in 1-8.[44]

1945 Henry's first son, Arthur R. Smith, died. The only child of Hannah Smith, he is located in 4-432-4.

August 9, 1945 *Wichita Eagle* Article: Tax lien auction (for 1910 paving of Hillside) along with the Old Mission Cemetery. Old Mission was owned and operated by Quiring Mortuary, who also leased Highland at the time.[45]

---

[44] ibid, August 1935
[45] Wichita Eagle, August 9, 1945

1948 letter: Sometime before this letter was written, C. V. Coble replaced Mr. Baird as Supervisor of Highland, for the Lot Owner's Association.[46]

1949 New Wichita Cemetery Company Lot Owners' board elected: W. Sternberg, President; H. Darling, Mable Criner, John Davidson, Jr (former president 1935-49) and G. Munn.

Mr. Darling is located in 4-250 and Ms. Criner is located in 3-323.

1951 Wichita Cemetery Company Lot Owners' board elected: H. Darling, President; A. Price, Treasurer; and M. Criner, Secretary.

1952-53 Wichita Cemetery Company elected board: Harry Stanley, President; H. Darling, Treasurer; and Mable Criner, Secretary.

Harry Stanley was the grandfather of Melodee Stanley Eby. His wife was Blanche Imboden Stanley, who is located in 4-61-4.

---

[46] October 13, 1948 Letter from W. C. Glenns, to Frank Stevens. Courtesy First Presbyterian Church, Gary Huffman, Archivist.

In 1953-54, four ladies of the First Presbyterian Church rewrote the records of Highland Cemetery, which dated "back to 1868."[47]

> Miss Bessie Goodyear, daughter of Emma and Charles
>
> Mrs. Irene Harrod, daughter of Mary and George Robinson
>
> Mrs. May Morris, daughter of Cynthia and P. L. Arnett
>
> Miss Harriet E Stanley, daughter of Emma and W. E. Stanley.

(Harriet Stanley was also the great aunt of Melodee Stanley Eby.)

1955 Wichita Cemetery Company Lot Owner's elected board: Harry Stanley, President; George Brown, Treasurer; and Mable Criner, Secretary.

Mr. Brown is located in the mausoleum. Mr. Stanley and Ms. Criner are located in the cemetery.

In 1958, under the leadership of Harry Stanley,

> *"the cemetery association approached the county with an agreement: If the county maintenance crews would keep the roads in good shape, the cemetery would maintain the graves on Potter's Field. Mrs. Quiring...followed with a second suggestion: citizens would donate...to purchase a chain link fence around the cemetery, if the county would install it."*[48]

March 15, 1964 Article with interview with Mrs. Quiring describes how Quiring came into the management of the cemetery. She also discovered who is responsible for maintenance in certain areas of the cemetery. For

---

[47] Email from Gary Huffman, March 31, 2016; Letter from 1953.
[48] Wichita Sunday Eagle, March 15, 1964.

example, since the county was in ownership of a part of the cemetery, they were and are still responsible for upkeep of the roads at Highland.[49]

August 31, 1965 The Highland Mausoleum Association was legally dissolved. However, in 1975 two meetings of the Mausoleum Association were held to discuss selling land in front of the mausoleum for profit. It was found that first of all, the association did not own the land. Second, the land was left empty for decorative purposes, and could not be used for burials.

The Highland Mausoleum board members were:

> Finley Ross Little
>
> Melodee Stanley Eby
>
> Mary Brown
>
> Hunter Gilkeson, Jr.

1982 Highland Cemetery was formally abandoned by the lot owner's association. Per Kansas State Annotated Statue 13-14c01, the jurisdiction where the cemetery is located is required to take it over when abandoned. Neil Vyff was the city superintendent when the City received the cemetery.

A Quit Claim was conveyed to the city on Dec 29, 1982. The City Council approved the action on January 11, 1983 and the deed was recorded January 18, 1983. Hunter Gilkeson, Jr was the President of the Wichita Cemetery Company at the time the deed was conveyed to the City.

---

[49] Wichita Eagle and Beacon, March 15, 1964.

1982 The Historic Wichita Board was assigned to have oversight of the cemetery. That Board was dissolved in 1987. The city is now responsible for maintaining the grass and trees, and the county is responsible for the roads.[50]

As of 1982, plots cannot be purchased for burials in Highland. The only burials in the cemetery are for family members of people who already purchased plots.

November 1987 Article about the history of Highland and Maple Grove cemeteries.[51]

1989 Jamesburg Cemetery was officially abandoned. Four cemeteries are now owned and maintained by the city of Wichita: Highland, the Wichita Mausoleum (at Highland,) Jamesburg and the Old Mission Mausoleum.

Painting of Wichita Mausoleum by Bill Goffrier, 2018.

---

[50]City Park website, accessed Sept 29, 2015
[51] Wichita Eagle and Beacon, November 15, 1987

Taken in the early 1990s, Bev Henline is shown here in costume for a historical tour led by the First Presbyterian Church's archivist Al Witherspoon. Characters were often provided by Cowtown for these reenactment tours.[52]

May 1995 Article about the recent vandalisms at Highland. There had been nearly 200 stones vandalized by that time, and the article cites common times for vandalisms as Memorial Day and Halloween. As a result, the city Park Department locks the Cemetery every year on Halloween, to deter from such damage.[53]

---

[52] Carol Peterson, photographer. Courtesy First Presbyterian Church.
[53] Wichita Eagle, May 29, 1995

August 1995 Interview about Henry Smith by Beccy Tanner with his grandson, Elmer. He remembered having been at the farmhouse as a child.[54]

1998 Cowtown's "Sagacity" article about the history of Highland and Maple Grove Cemeteries, by Eric Cale. The article was also shared on Maple Grove's website.

May 2004 "The Wichita Mausoleum" article regarding Dr. Richard Ferrell's great grandfather, Lloyd Bascom Ferrell. Mr. Ferrell is in the mausoleum which Dr. Ferrell wanted made into a local landmark. A picture of the mausoleum was part of the article.[55]

July 2004 Letter from David Holmes, Dr. Richard Ferrell's attorney, regarding the mausoleum's ownership. A large amount of legal discovery was compiled in 2004 for this purpose.

2005-2012 The Ark Valley Crossroads reported on the "Highland Cemetery Project" as one of their special interest projects. Claudia Vickery of the Wichita Genealogical Society was the author of the articles each quarter.

2007 Bill Pennington recorded all of the burials in Highland, making a full spreadsheet that he then shared with the city Park Department, Midwest Historical Genealogical Society, Wichita Public Library and local museums. The spreadsheet is now available on the website: ksgenweb.org.

---

[54] Wichita Eagle, August 10, 1995.
[55] Ibid, May 2, 2004.

2012 Article about six grave stones found in Haysville.[56] Since both Findagrave and Face book were fairly new programs, and not widely used yet, finding the owners so quickly was extraordinary!

STONES FOUND IN DITCH TIED TO WICHITA CEMETERY

Six old headstones were found by a Sedgwick County sheriff's deputy while on patrol Monday in the 12th block of West 67th Street South. The stones were tracked via the Internet to Highland Cemetery at Ninth and Hillside in Wichita. The mystery now is who took them.

Headstones hold mystery

June 4, 2015 KAKE online article about the mother of Lilley Willis, who is buried at Highland, and about family's concern about the disrepair there.

May 2016 *Wichita Eagle* article interviews with Jami Frazier-Tracy, Bill Pennington, David Stuart and Barb Myers.[57]

November 8, 2016 The Friends of the Wichita Pioneers incorporated.

---

[56] Wichita Eagle, February 21, 2012. This would be the first preservation project for the Friends of the Wichita Pioneers, Inc. in 2017.
[57] Ibid, May 27, 2016.

May 2017 City of Wichita took legal ownership of the mausoleum. The City Park and City Facilities departments take care of the building and grounds.

2017 The City of Wichita made the records of burials at Highland openly available on their city park website.

As of May 2018, there have been about 17,250 burials at Highland.

In 1988, The Historical Wichita Board posted a plaque with the names of fifteen influential Wichitans buried at Highland, and a map of the cemetery on the maintenance building at the front of the cemetery.

CHAPTER FOUR:

Friends of the Wichita Pioneers, Inc.

"Be the change you wish to see in the world." - (Mahatma Gandhi)

2014

Barb Myers began research and tours.

August - Her first visit to Highland. This visit gave her the resolution to care for the cemetery and it's "residents".

October – "Walkabouts" of downtown and other parts of Wichita, to get a feel for the history of the city, and why the people at Highland were important to remember.

The author's mother, Mary Myers at the grave of William "Buffalo Bill" Mathewson, October 2014.

2015

March 15, 2015 The first tour was given, for two of Barb's friends. The next tour was on October 17, 2015, with nearly 50 in attendance.

May – "Wichita History From My Perspective" Facebook page starts, to share what is found. The group currently has over 13,500 members!

Powerline guy-wire in Potter's Field removed from the grave of Elizabeth Henderson.

Picture of Elizabeth Henderson's (PF-7-4E) and Ruby Dice's (PF-7-5E) markers.

The post was almost 6-feet long! Luckily, it was diagonal, and didn't impede on any graves.

2016

April – Over 100 attended the historical tour.

May – *Wichita Eagle* Article.

July – Wichitalks, *Sunflower*, KWCH and KAKE articles.

Because of flooding, a new culvert was added in block 2 by the City.

Began Mausoleum tours and Memorial Day/Christmas Day mausoleum duty.

All three shirts we have sold as fund raisers.

Incorporation: Nov. 8, 2016

2017

February – By cutting four trees down in block 3, 27-markers from the Cogdell and Tarlton families were uncovered by the City Forestry Department.

March - First "Work Day." We replaced the Steele childrens', Birtie Summers', Mary Dawson's, Joseph Mohan's and Timothy Joseph O'Conner's stones, which had been recovered in 2012. Preservation was finished in May.

April 5 and June 5 – Barb did interviews at KPTS ("Positively Kansas") with Jim Grawe, about progress at the cemetery. Interviews number 2 (April 5) and 10 (June 5) can be seen on YouTube.

Summer – Give-back fundraiser nights at Delano BBQ, ChickfilA and Chipotle.

October - Halloween themed historical tour.

October and November - Historical bus tours given as fund raisers for the Highland Ce

metery.

May 2017 - Proclamation made by the Kansas State Senate.

Barb Myers, Chairperson of the Friends of the Wichita Pioneers with Kansas State Senator Lynn Rogers, Memorial Day weekend, 2017. Proclamation received in recognition of the work completed by the Friends of the Wichita Pioneers committee at Highland.

New logo design, by Dalton Sanders.

2018

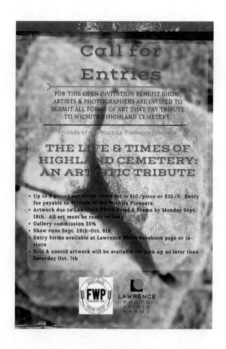

Call for
Entries

FOR THIS OPEN INVITATION BENEFIT SHOW,
ARTISTS & PHOTOGRAPHERS ARE INVITED TO
SUBMIT ALL FORMS OF ART THAT PAY TRIBUTE
TO WICHITA'S HIGHLAND CEMETERY.

Friends of the Wichita Pioneers present

THE LIFE & TIMES OF
HIGHLAND CEMETERY:
AN ARTISTIC TRIBUTE

- Up to 3 pieces per artist, entry fee is $10/piece or $25/3. Entry fee payable to Friends of the Wichita Pioneers.
- Artwork due to Lawrence Photo Print & Frame by Monday Sept. 18th. All art must be ready to hang.
- Gallery commission 35%
- Show runs Sept. 28th-Oct. 6th
- Entry forms available at Lawrence Photo Facebook page or in-store
- Sold & unsold artwork will be available for pick up no later than Saturday Oct. 7th

FWP   LAWRENCE
           PHOTO
           PRINT &
           FRAME

This was a photo Contest and art show sponsored by Lawrence Photography. Fundraiser for the Friends of the Wichita Pioneers.

We have completed around 300 markers' cleaning, repair and preservation as of July 2018. We have received over 500 approvals, many of which are still waiting to be completed.

Some of the Friends of the Wichita Pioneers volunteers, working on one of the many projects completed at Highland Cemetery. (Yes, FWP owns a jackhammer!)

Before.

After.

The base of the Johnston family's marker was replaced by the Friends of the Wichita Pioneers in the Spring of 2018.

CHAPTER FIVE:

Abode of the Dead

TO **I. W. GILL,** DR.
UNDERTAKER AND EMBALMER.

OFFICE TELEPHONE 102.
RESIDENCE 'PHONE 250.

327 EAST DOUGLAS AVENUE.

July 28 To Black Cloth Casket $75.00
" Washing & Shaving 5.00
" Embalming Body 25.00
" Burial Robe 8.00
" Hearse & Service 10.00 $123.00

The purpose of this chapter is not to put any person who is buried at Highland before any other person in terms of importance. Nor is it to recreate the recorded biographies in books such as William G. Cutler's (1883,) Chapman Brothers (1888,) or Orsemus Hills Bentley's (1910.) All of those are valuable for historical research. That is why I have listed deaths chronologically.

What follows is bits of stories that the descendants of those at Highland have shared with me. I have also included the founding of other cemeteries, mortuaries and churches, for frame of reference.

Per Bill Pennington's research, some of the confirmed burials before 1870 include:

Fanny E. Crow (1856). Located in 3-75.

Louella McCampbell (1862.) Located in 2-61.

Julia Deming (1862.) Located in 1-252.

Mary Sweeney (1864.) Located in 2-119.

Martha Eggleston (1867.) Located in 1-307.[58]

Albert Lewellen (1868.) Located in 1-42.

Otia English (1868.) Located in 1-53.

Etta Smith (1869.) Located in 3-5.

Kent Tanner (1869.) Located in 4-368.

Of note: There is a plot number given for each of the above, so it is important to remember that the cemetery was not platted yet when these individuals died. Space numbers would have been irrelevant at the time.

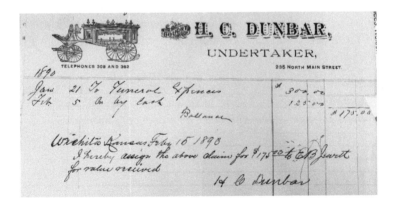

---

[58] Martha died in Mississippi in 1867, but her husband brought her body and the body of their son to Kansas in 1876 for reburial.

1868 Otia English, one-year old daughter of Nathaniel, died. She is buried with the family, in 1-53. [59]

The post in front of the grave marker is from the Chisholm Trail 150th Anniversary committee, in recognition of English's status as a founder of Wichita. There are at least eight at Highland and several more at Maple Grove Cemetery.

1868 Young Albert Lewellen died. His mother Susanah (Doc Lewellen's first wife) died in 1872. Two of Albert's sisters, Hannah Ward (in 3-142-5) and Emma Slyter (in 4-12-4), are also buried at Highland.

---

[59] Episcopal Church history book

Albert is located at 1-42-8 and his mother is nearby.

INTERESTING FACT:

Doc's real name was Doctor! It was said that his father, Zadock, wanted a doctor in the family, so he named one of his sons that. Mr. Lewellen operated the first store in Wichita in 1868, in what had been Chisholm's eastern most trading post. Lewellen then moved back to El Dorado and remarried, to Delilah. Doc had 12 children, with his two wives.[60]

This stone faces west. His mother's memorial on the south side of the same stone.

The Slyters are on the east and the Stices, more family, are on the south.

In 1869, Rev. Wilberforce Boggs started preaching to the first Presbyterian church congregation. In 1870, the First Presbyterian Church was chartered and met with Rev. Boggs in a dugout at 12th and Jackson. The 13 charter members include: William Finn, Ellen Boggs, John Steele, Edward Peck and his wife Margaret and their daughters Annie

---

[60] City of Chelsea history book

and Mary, William Smith, Lucy Greenway, B. S. Dunbar, William Gill, Robert Bowes and Amy Sayles. The first installed preacher was Rev. John Pease Harsen. Their first church was built in 1870 and was sold to the Catholics in 1872. This building was sold to Millie Hodge in 1886 and was known as the Hotel Centropolis (Hodge) boarding house until 1948. It is now restored back to its appearance as First Presbyterian Church and is located at Cowtown.

The Episcopal church started the same year, with the Rev. John Price Hilton holding services at the Munger home. The first church was built at 400 N Main. The 18 charter members include Charley Hunter, Darius Munger, Henry Vigus, Milo Kellogg, Nathaniel English, James R. Mead, Edwin B. Allen, James Black, William B. Hutchinson, William Baldwin, Charley Schattner, Phares Hubbard, the Aleys, the Harris' and the Fishers.

August 29, 1870 Frank Allen, son of druggist (pharmacist) Joseph P. Allen[61] died at 2 months old. He was the first white child born in Wichita.[62] Frank was buried on land donated by the Wichita Town Company. Frank is located in 1-2-9. His father Joseph is in 1-2-5.

---

[61] Later, Joseph was Wichita's 9th Mayor. Joseph's brother was Dr. Edwin B. Allen, Wichita' 1st Mayor and 2nd doctor.
[62] One could say that saying "first" is semantics. "In Wichita" infers AFTER 1870. Sedgwick County was not founded until later the same year. Before that, the area to the East of the cemetery was Butler County, and to the North was Otoe county. But people were here, lived here and died here before 1870.

Feb. 28, 1871 John E. "Jack" Ledford was killed by two Army soldiers, for having stolen two mules to satisfy a debt he felt he was owed by the Army. Ironically, he still had a military burial.[63]

His 16-year old wife Alice Harris was the step daughter of Henry Vigus. Jack owned the Wichita (or Harris, named after his wife) Hotel. He is located in 1-96-6.

INTERESTING FACTs:

Jack Ledford was elected Sheriff in 1871, but never served.

After his death, Alice married Elder Fred Martsolf, of the Presbyterian Church (she was from the Episcopal church), and they later moved to Pittsburgh, PA. She was hit by a train and died soon after and was buried there.[64]

Ledford's original gravestone. (Image courtesy Cowtown.) Note: His middle initial was actually E.

---

[63] Cutler, part 3.

[64] Sagacity article; Bentley 1910 book, pages 6, 9, 174; First Presbyterian Church, Gary Huffman Archivist; Sedgwick County Sheriff history book, pages 12-13; Beccy Tanner's book.

This is actually Ledford's second stone.

Note: The stone says he was in the MD Infantry. He was actually in the MO infantry. His middle initial is also E, not H.

1871 Mike Meagher was hired as City Marshal, and his brother John was hired as Sheriff.

1871 First jail (or calaboose) was built on the SW corner of Market and 2nd, by Ludlum and Lindsay Const. After being moved, and eventually owned by the school district, the building was moved to Cowtown in 1952.

The jail located at Central and Market was designed by C. W. Fisk in 1874. Fisk is buried in 1-192.[65]

1871 Thomas Sullivan (1796-1871; in 2-59-7) died. He was one of three people buried at Highland who were born in the 1700s. Mary Minsker

[65] USD 259 School District history book

(1797-1887; in 1-177-11) and Maria Long (1799-1885; in 3-164-7) were the other two

.

1871 Timothy Meagher died from palsy. From Ireland, his three daughters were Celia Steele, Ellen Mohan and Elizabeth O'Conner. All three had children buried at Highland. Timothy's sons were Mike and John who both served in law enforcement. The family is located in 1-17.

INTERESTING FACTs:

Fr. Paul Ponziglione had 12 stations in Kansas, one of which was Wichita (another was the Osage Reservation.) The first time he came to Wichita was in 1869. The first mass was held at Mr. Meagher's home. The first Catholics in Wichita were the Meaghers, Mahaneys, and Catherine Greiffenstein and her son. By Nov. 27, 1870, there were 60 Catholics in the Wichita parish.

In 1872, Fr. Ponziglione appointed Mrs. Ellen Meagher to collect subscriptions for a new building. The lot was donated by James.R. Mead, and the first church building was bought from the Presbyterian Church (also previously known as the Centropolis (Hodge) Boarding House). The first Catholic church was then known as St. Aloysius.

In his travels, Fr. Ponziglione was almost a victim of the Benders![66]

1871 Ride of the Four Horsemen – James R Mead, Nathaniel English, Mike Meagher and John Marion "Big Jim" Steele met with Major Shanklin to convince him to come back through Wichita, instead of going straight north on the cattle trail. This decision would positively affect the future of Wichita.

---

[66] The Benders were a family from western Kansas. It was discovered later that they were luring travelers into their home and killed many. Fr. Ponziglione was in the home, and got a weird feeling, so he left in a hurry! History of the Wichita Catholic Diocese, page 25-26, 34.

1871 The death of the child of a Wichita settler, as told to the *Wichita Eagle* in 1920:

> *Among the many stout-hearted youths who came to Sedgwick county in 1871, and homesteaded, were John Ferman, age 21, and his boyhood friend, Ed Wall. The took claims adjoining in Illinois Township where Clonwell (sic) now stands, building a shanty on the dividing line and occupying it the required number months while "proving up" and worked for neighboring farmers while not so occupied.*

> *About the first of July of this year they were both employed by a Mr. Cook, Sr, northeast of Wichita. Mr. Cook's 18-month-old baby died and Mr. Fermin and a **brother** of Mr. Cook, Bob Cook, volunteered to dig the grave in Wichita's first cemetery, now called Highland Cemetery.*

> *At that time the vicinity of Highland Cemetery was covered with grass that grew higher than the men's heads and horse weeds and sunflowers that grew higher than the heads of horses, so they became lost. They had started about two o'clock, expecting to dig the grave and return in time to bury the baby that afternoon. They finally located the cemetery and dug the grave by the light of the moon while the howling of coyotes made them lonesome and gave them a weird feeling. They had no way to locate the cemetery except by a few posts and one wire surrounding the plot of ground set aside for that purpose, making it necessary for the men to be sure that they were digging the grave inside the prescribed place and not in some field.*

> *In the meantime, the father of the baby became very much alarmed for the safety of the two men and with Mr. Wall, started out to search for them just as they were returning. They buried the baby the next day and a wooden marker was placed at the head of the tiny grave. But it was not to stand long, for a short time later a prairie fire swept the country and the marker was burned. No record is found in the Highland cemetery books of this burial.[67]*

---

[67] Wichita Beacon, December 19, 1920.

I am still trying to figure where this baby would be. The Cook family is in 3-96 and in 3-6. From this narrative, she could be in either one.

Mr. Marshall John Ferman (1851-1919) is buried in 4-151-3,

INTERESTING FACT:

The Cook family owned the land where Wesley Hospital now stands. It was northeast of Wichita 'way out in Butler County' before Sedgwick County was formed!

Image: courtesy Dalton Sanders, 2018.

Maple Grove   Highland Cemetery
Founded 1888   Founded 1868

1872 Wichita becomes a city of the 2nd class with a population of 2,000.

1872 After Susanah Lewellen died, Doc moved back to Chelsea (a town that is now located under El Dorado Lake).

1872 Marshall Murdock was invited to come to Wichita. In April, after closing down his paper, the Osage County Chronicle, he came to Wichita and started publishing *The Wichita Eagle* weekly. Marshall's brother Roland was the business manager.

1872 *The Beacon* began daily publication in October. D. J. Millison was the owner and Frederick A. Sowers, previously the owner of *The Wichita Vidette* was the editor and manager.

It was a Democrat paper until Henry J. Allen bought it in 1907. In 1928, the Levands came to Wichita. Max and Louis purchased *The Beacon*, and John was the publisher. They owned the paper until it was sold to the Murdock family in 1960. Louis and Max's family are buried at the Jewish cemetery at Highland, Section 17.

The Sowers' family marker was broken into pieces and was laying on the ground. We put the entire marker back together, and cleaned it thoroughly.

The story of Frederick A. Sowers is recorded on his gravestone.

October 8, 1872 Eliza L. Flanders-Day died. She was the great grandmother of Sandra Day O'Connor.

Eliza was married to Hollis Day, and the family was only in Wichita for about two years. During that time, Mrs. Day died. Their son, H. C. married Alice E. Hilton, daughter of Rev. John Price Hilton and moved to Albuquerque, NM. Their son Harry married Ada, who soon had their daughter Sandra.

This would also make Rev. Hilton the maternal great-grandfather of Sandra. He was the preacher of the St. John's Episcopal Church in early Wichita.[68]

---

[68] St. James Episcopal Church history; *Lazy B-Growing up on a Cattle Ranch in the*

Eliza Flanders Day is buried alone, in 1-4-4.

1872 Rev Wilberforce Boggs died.   He was sent to Wichita from Emporia in 1869-to organize the First Presbyterian Church in Wichita. In 1870, he used William Finn's abandoned Army dugout-school for the church (which was at what is now 12th and Jackson.) He had left Wichita for the city of Oxford by 1871, when Rev. John Pease Harsen became the first installed pastor of 30 members. Boggs, his wife Ellen and their son Paul are located in 2-182.

1872 Mary Peck Smith, wife of William Smith[69], died in childbirth.

Mary Peck and her family were founding members of the First Presbyterian Church, as was William. Mary and William had the first marriage held at First Presbyterian Church.

Mary and her infant are located in 4-288, next to Joshua and Mary Smith, parents of William. First Presbyterian Church installed a stone on her grave in 1991.[70]

American Southwest; O'Connor, Sandra Day and H. Alan Day, Random House; New York, 2002.
[69] Step-brother of Henry Smith.
[70] Sedgwick County Sheriff history book, vol 1.; Wichita Century, page 41.

THE FIRST PRESBYTERIAN
CHURCH OF WICHITA
ESTABLISHED 1869

DUGOUT WHERE FIRST
SERVICES WERE HELD

FIRST PERMANENT
CHURCH STRUCTURE

MARY PECK AND WILLIAM SMITH
WERE THE FIRST COUPLE MARRIED IN THE
CHURCH BOTH WERE CHARTER MEMBERS
THIS MEMORIAL WAS DONATED BY THE
WOMEN OF THE FIRST PRESBYTERIAN
CHURCH IN 1992

The story of the Smiths is engraved on the back of her marker.

The First Presbyterian Church installed the marker in 1992.

October 27, 1873 Edward F. "Red" Beard was killed by Rowdy Joe Lowe on Douglas Street, just west of the bridge. He staggered into the street and died on the bridge.[71] Beard is located in 1-110 in an unmarked grave next to his wife Deborah. His daughter Clara Beard-Garrett-Jones is buried in 2-50-3.

Beard's probate file is an interesting look at Wichita history. His will was dated April 8, 1873, just months before his death.

---

[71] Cutler, Part 3.

His is the earliest receipt I found written by Henry Smith.

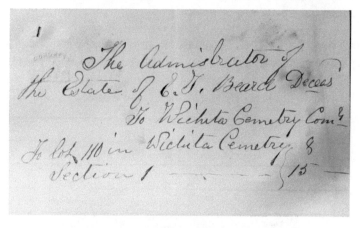

In "lot 110, section 1."

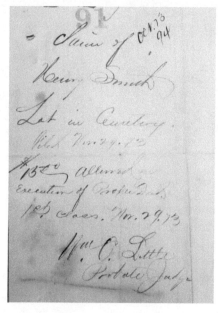

The $15.00 for Beard's plot was paid by his estate.

Rowdy Joe Lowe was apprehended by Sheriff William Smith.

1874 Young Willie A. Richey died. His grave stone was found in a yard near Wesley Hospital in 2017. Our group repaired the stone and returned it to Highland. However, a new one had already been installed. So, now Willie has two markers. He and his family are located in 3-208-9.

1874 Lucy Greenway, member of the Cherokee tribe (she was one quarter Cherokee) died. Lucy arrived in Wichita in 1869 and was a founding member of the First Presbyterian Church. Her husband, town founder and former ferry operator Andrew (sometimes known as AJ, AF or H) moved with their two children Alonzo and Minnie to Indian territory. Two of their children (John and Jeanette) are buried at Highland with her. Her stone was donated by the First Presbyterian Church in 1991. She is located in 3-40-11 next to her youngest two children.

Front.

The story of Lucy Greenway is engraved on the back of her marker.

The First Presbyterian Church installed her marker in 1991.

In 1875, Officer Wyatt Earp got into a fist fight with William Smith (who didn't like Earp's family.) Smith was then a candidate for county sheriff. Earp was fired and left for Dodge City soon after.[72]

1875 Kendle Undertaking (and sewing machines and cabinets) founded by Hiram W. Kendle. Cabinet makers were often also undertakers.

1876 A cemetery land deed was sold to African American, Mrs. Maria Robinson for a family plot 4-105.[73]

The line in the contract showing the cost is illegible.

---

[72] Wichita Daily Eagle, April 21, 1875; Ibid, April 19, 1876.

[73] Four generations from Richard is Gerald Robinson, who was married to Frances Waller Tomlin. Frances was three generations down from Ruben Waller, a Buffalo Soldier in the Civil War. His story is told on the Kansas State Historical Society website, Kansapedia. The Waller family has a very, long proud history in law enforcement as well. Judge Greg Waller was the judge in the Dennis Rader/BTK case. (I knew other members of their family—great-great grandson Kobe Ford went to school with my daughter, in Haven, KS.)

Richard Robinson was the only African American signer of the Wichita City charter in 1870. In 1896, his son George W. Robinson began working for the Wichita Fire Department and later became the first African American fire captain. He started a century long family tradition in fire safety. George died in 1964, in the Robinson family plot.

1877 Greenwood Cemetery in Oatville founded. This was a town on the Chisholm Trail, and the town in which Emma Goodyear and Mary Mossman lived before coming to Wichita.

1877 Whitecotton (aka, "Lutheran:") Cemetery's first burial. It is located at 45th and Hillside.

1877 Sunnydale existed unincorporated until 1901. This was the area in which the Masterson family lived.

1877 Wichita had a scarlet fever epidemic. There are 11 deaths from scarlet fever in Highland.[74]

INTERESTING FACT:

Did you know that picnics were held in cemeteries until about 1926 so that people could be closer to their loved ones?[75]

---

[74] First Presbyterian Church's death records show who died and when in those years, as records were not required to be kept by counties.
[75] FPC history records, Gary Huffman Archivist

March 1877 Three children of city founder John Marion "Big Jim" Steele (Eliza, born 1873; Henry, born 1874; and Timothy, born 1875) died from Scarlet fever within three weeks.

While in Wichita, John was on the Town Council, the first County Commission, was the Sedgwick County Clerk and was a member of the State Legislature. Big Jim, his wife Celia (sister of Mike Meagher) and one son moved to Tacoma, WA in 1881, the next town John helped found. He died in Tacoma, in 1896. His children are located in 1-17.

Before repairs.

The restored grave marker for the Steele children. (Several parts had to be rebuilt by the Friends of the Wichita Pioneers in 2017.)

1877 Betsy Tramblie died. She was the third wife of Jonas Tramblie. We unearthed her headstone and cornerstones while looking for a nearby headstone. She is buried alone in 1-40-5.

1877 Charles Alliston, husband of Blanche (daughter of Robert S. Cook), died. (Pam Good's family, and a member of the Cook family.) He is located in 3-10, near the Cook family.

1877 Carrie Redfield died of Scarlet fever. A cherry tree fell on her marker in 2017. Raymond Downing's family approved its repair after the city cut the tree out.

Damages, after the cherry tree fell.

After repairs.

Miss Redfield is located near her parents, Josiah and Carrie H. in 3-35.[76] The rest of their family is buried in Humboldt, KS.

James Cairns, brother in law of Bat Masterson, became Marshal on March 11, 1879.

December 5, 1879 City founder (the Wichita Town Company's 'advance man') Darius S. Munger died. He was the postmaster from 1870-1874; was elected coroner from 1876-78; co-managed the Empire House; and allowed several churches to use his home when needed. The funeral drew around 800 people!

Darius' wife Julia Phelps Munger and their daughter Julia Richards are also buried at Highland. The family is located in 3-47. (His other two daughters are buried elsewhere.)

---

[76] Ark Valley Crossroads article written by Raymond Downing. Vol 18, #3, July 2007.

The Munger's family marker.

In 1947, after being sold and renovated several times, the Munger's home was moved by the Eunice Sterling Chapter of the Daughters of the American Revolution to the land that is now Cowtown. The first house in Wichita, it was built in 1868 and originally located at what is now 9th and Waco. The home had also been owned by W. C. Woodman and was known as Lakeside Mansion at the time.

1879 Allyn Lawrence died. He is located in 1-10.

Allyn's father Henry (a former Justice of the Peace) and mother Abigail are buried nearby. The arch shaped marker next to the larger family marker is for two of Robert's children (Allyn's brother.)

INTERESTING FACTs:

Allyn's brother Charles started Lawrence Drug Store in 1877. He sold photography equipment out of the drugstore until 1888, when he made a deal with George Eastman to be the sole salesperson of Eastman's cameras in Wichita. By 1900, Charles had closed the drug store and just ran Lawrence Photography. Charles died in a traffic accident in 1932. He is buried at Maple Grove.

Their brother was Robert E. Lawrence. Robert also had a son Charles, who was Wichita's 32nd and 36th mayor, and is interred at Highland Cemetery's mausoleum. Robert died in 1911 and is buried at Maple Grove.

1879 Calvin P. Pearson died. He is located in 3-46 with his family. His children's markers are unique: They are metal with painted glass fronts.

1880 Charles M. Platt died. Interestingly, he is a white man and is buried with two small children, in the middle of a mainly African American area of block 4. They are located in 4-104.

1881 Mike Meagher (pronounced Ma-har) was killed in Caldwell.

Mike Meagher was born in Ireland in 1844 and came with his family to America in 1848. He and his brother John moved to Salina in 1867 and to Wichita in 1868. They hauled lumber to Wichita for Darius Munger's house and decided to stay. Mike was the city marshal 1871-76 (except 1874-75 when William Smith was the marshal). Mike hired Wyatt Earp and James Cairns at the same time. (Interestingly, Cairns was Bat Masterson's brother in law. Also, of note, Cairns became the Sheriff in 1879.)

Mike married Jennie Hitchcock in 1873 and moved to Caldwell in 1878, becoming Caldwell's mayor thereafter. Even though not in law enforcement at the time, he was killed while assisting in an arrest. Mike was shot by J. M. Talbot in 1881. It was widely thought that his brother avenged his murder later, and then moved to South Dakota.

Mike is buried in 1-17-10 near his father, and several nieces and nephews.[77]

Mike Meagher's stone has been cleaned.

[77] Kansapedia, Kansas State Historical Society webpage. Accessed June 23, 2018.

1881 Adda Brown died. The Browns, located in 2-134, are the family of LeeAnn Sack and Esther Herrington.

1881 Susan A. Jones Toler died. Grandmother of Sidney Toler, aka "Charlie Chan." There are seven family members located in 4-145.

Susan's marker.

Harriet (Hattie I. Quarles) Vigus, mother of Alice Harris, died in 1871. She is buried 'on the prairie.' Land that her husband, Henry Vigus owned is about where 21st and Main are now, so that is most likely where she is buried.[78]

[78] Episcopal Church history; History from First Presbyterian Church, Gary Huffman Archivist.

Grave marker of Henry Vigus.

His second wife Hattie (he actually had two wives with the name Hattie,) died in 1880 and is thought to be buried next to him at Highland, in an unmarked grave.

Henry owned the Buckhorn Saloon at the time Wichita began, and was a founding member of the Episcopal church. He died on April 11, **1882** and is located in 3-41.

1883 Hoss Cemetery (aka, Maple Grove, near what is now Park City) founded.[79] Per Vince Marshall, it was NOT segregated.

1883 Abbie J. Lawrence, child of Robert E. Lawrence died. She and her brother Freddie are located in 1-10 with their grandparents and Uncle Allyn.

---

[79] Vince Marshall, Ark Valley News March 25, 2010; Roadside Thoughts website; Digital Valley Center, August 1, 2016.

1884 Salt mine owner Thomas McCampbell died. He is located with his family in 2-6

December 23, 1884 Rebecca Hilton died after a fall. Her parents had the Hilton Plaster Co. The family is located in 4-320.

1885 Kansas counties were required to keep their own death records on file, instead of relying upon undertakers and mortuaries to do so.

1885 Early African American business owner Wesley Hodge died. He had been a blacksmith, and after his death his wife Millie operated the Hotel Centropolis boarding house in the former First Presbyterian Church/St. Aloysius Catholic Church.

The family is located in the north half of plot 4-365. The plots cost Millie $12.00, which was recorded in 1886.

Millie's sister's husband is at Highland, but her sister Fannie, is not.

November 1885 Anna Arnstein died, necessitating a Jewish Cemetery in Wichita. That year, the Congregation Emanu-El purchased the land where the Jewish cemetery at Highland is located.

1885 Harry Ham died. His wife Hattie remarried into the Johnston and Teague family (who are located in 2-217.) He is located in 1-83 with Hattie.

1886 John G. Hope, a Wichita druggist (pharmacist,) and the 2nd and 4th Mayor of Wichita, died. He is located in 1-267-1.

1887 Adolph Wiegand died. He was shown as a brewer on the 1885 census, at a time when there was prohibition in Wichita! He is located in 4-4-3.

1887 Two-year old Loyd Gray, an African American, is located in 1-85-7. He is one of only six African Americans in block 1.

1887 Mike Zimmerly, City Council member and real estate developer died.[80] His wife completed the building of the Zimmerly Block in downtown Wichita, in 1897.

---

[80] Chapman 1888, page 531-32.

Zimmerly and his family are located in 1-305-11, by one of the tallest markers at Highland. It is near, and resembles, William Mathewson's marker.

INTERESTING FACT:

When Zimmerly died, A. A. Hyde was named his estate administrator.

After the "bust" of 1899, the block was purchased by Scott Winne, who absconded with a large amount of mortgage funds from Wichita in 1908. The building was then sold to a Mr. Watt, and then Mr. Street. The building, at 210 E. Douglas, was razed in 2016, and the Douglas Apartments are in that location now

1887 Richard B. Tarlton died of typhoid/malaria. A Confederate officer, he was the first husband of Caroline, who later became William Mathewson's second wife. Tarlton's grave was found under four largely overgrown trees, which were removed in 2017. (There were 27 graves under those trees!)

Tarlton is located next to Richard Cogdell, a fellow Confederate officer, in 3-28 and the Bitting family in 3-13, and the trees were in between.

1887 Julia Deming died. Her daughter Julia, was Mrs. R. C. Israel; and her daughter Mary was Mrs. Charles W. Bitting. Mrs. Deming is located next to her husband in 1-252.

1887 Dr. Henry O. Burleigh died. He was responsible for building St. Francis Hospital in 1880 and Wesley Hospital soon after. He and his family are located in 3-173.[81]

---

[81] Chapman p. 709-710; Wichita Eagle, January 4, 1888

1887 Cordelia Root died. She was the wife of Russell E. Root. She is located in 3-54 with four of her children.[82]

1887 Calvary Baptist Church founded.

1888 Maple Grove Cemetery founded.

1888 Calvary Cemetery founded by the Wichita Catholic Diocese.

1889 Mueller Funeral Home founded.

1889 Henry Lawrence, father of Robert, Charles and Allyn died. He is located in 1-10.

■■

Before and After:

Biological solutions such as D/2 should always be used instead of harsh cleaners. A non-abrasive soap and water are a good substitute, also. Never use vinegar!

---

[82] Chapman, p. 1104.

1890 Nelson McClees died. He was a Confederate Captain in Co. B of the North Carolina Light Artillery. In 1881 he bought the shaft being dug by Mr. Thomas McCampbell for coal, when salt water was found instead. McClees was on the school board from 1906-1909.

After a fall in which his thigh was broken, he quickly died. He and his family have the only free-standing mausoleum at Highland, which is in block 4.

The mausoleum cost $950.00 and his casket, $300.00.

1890 Abicenia Sullard died. She is buried with her family in 1-40, but there is no marker.

1891 Union Brevet Brigadier General Beroth B. Eggleston died. Gen. Eggleston was the General of the Ohio Volunteer Cavalry and settled in Mississippi in 1868. He ran for Governor in 1868 and while he did not win, he was active in Republican politics until 1876. That year he moved to Wichita, and when he did so, he brought the bodies of his wife and son

Edward who had died previously, for burial. Gen. and Mrs. Eggleston are located in 1-307 with their son, and daughter Laura Myers. His daughter Mary Charlton is located in 3-22 and his son Arthur is located in 1-249.

August 3, 1892 Nathaniel English died. He was chairman of the first County Commissioners, married to Osie, and was one of the Four Horsemen and founder of Wichita. He also named Douglas Street after his friend Senator Stephen A. Douglas. Mr. English is buried in 1-53-9.

INTERESTING FACT:

Mr. English had 12 children, including Margie Fuller and Kate English Smith. Margie's daughter Ella married Finlay Ross; her son Tom helped found Cowtown; and Kate's husband Alton founded Eastborough.

February 3, 1892. The strange court case surrounding the body of an unknown woman found at Maple Grove, which should not have been there. The undertaker, Mr. Kendle, did not want the body buried at Highland because he did not like Henry Smith, but ultimately the body was moved back to Highland anyway. During the trial, Kendle admitted to **procuring bodies** from Kansas City for the University of Embalming, where he was the president. Jacob McAfee and Henry Smith were jurors on the court case.[83]

August 1892 Mary (May?) McFrederick died of scarlet fever at age 15. Her father, John had a heart attack and died at the funeral. He is buried next to her in 4-237.[84]

Daughter.

Father.

---

[83] Wichita Daily Eagle, February 3, 1892
[84] Ibid, August 14, 1892.

November 1892 *Wichita Eagle* article.

> Henry Smith's "… *children told him that some man had entered the cemetery with a bundle whose strange actions had led them to believe that everything was not altogether right.*" [85]

Henry investigated and found that the body of an infant girl had recently been buried in a shallow grave there.

The second baby of Mr. and Mrs. Louis Miller died after being born prematurely, on November 17. The father accidently dug the hole in the grave of a man named Churchill, but the baby was eventually buried in 4-239 with a sibling who had died earlier that year. Joseph died on June 19 and daughter "L." died in October 14. The investigation was dismissed on December 2, 1892.

1893 Elijah W. Israel died. Father of R. C. Israel. R. C.'s sons Carl and Bob started the Boathouse. (Bob's son was involved with the formation of Cowtown.) Elijah is located in 4-38-10.[86]

[85] Ibid, November 30, 1892.
[86] Colwich Journal letter written by Mr. E. W. Israel after June 12, 1893.

Mr. Israel had express instructions to his family of how he wished to be buried. He wanted a simple stone (although about 6-feet tall) for a grave marker, a pine box, and to be wrapped in white sheet. If it was good enough for Jesus, it was what he wanted.

1893 The ornamental cannon was installed in the GAR section. It was dedicated by the Caroline Harrison circle of Daughters of the Union Veterans in 1921. The Eggleston post Grand Army of the Republic unit was in effect from 1894-1932. This was the women's auxiliary of that unit.

1894 Cook family patriarch Andrew J. Cook died. He is located in 3-6.[87] (Mr. Cook's casket cost $64.00.)

The Cooks, Munns and Sayles owned the land where Wesley Hospital is now. They were also founding members of the First Presbyterian Church.

---

[87] Cutler, 1888. Page 551.

1894 Lucy Inman Mead died. Her sister Elizabeth Inman Mathewson is buried at Highland. The second wife of James R. Mead, Lucy had previously been Mead's housekeeper and the caretaker of his small children (as Elizabeth had also done.) Lucy is located in 1-263-4. She had no children of her own.

The author with Dr. Schuyler Jones, grandson of James R. Mead, 2017. Dr. Jones's grandmother was J. R. Mead's 3rd wife, Fern.

1895 John Germen died. He served in the 6th ILL. Cavalry in the Civil War and was later a farmer in east Butler county (now, Sedgwick County.) His wife Sussana and son George are located near him in 3-15.

1895 Mrs. Henrietta Elizabeth McCracken-Riker-Condit died of cancer. Her service was held by the Salvation Army, and she is buried in 4-50-6B, the Salvation Army's plot. She left a 14-year old son.

1896 John Sawyer, architect of Turner Opera house and the Murdock house died. He is located in 1-149.

1896 Miles Shinn died. He is located next to his family, Alice and Newman, in 1-116. The stones have sunken.

December 1896 Body snatching of Mrs. A. M. Roll from the EP (GAR) section. There might have been two doctors involved. In EP-14-8, on the farthest SE corner of the cemetery, and there was no fence around Highland at the time.[88]

---

[88] National Reflector, January 1, 1896.

1898 United States involvement in the Spanish American War.

1898 Lewis Bitting died. Father of businessmen Charles and Alfred Bitting. Their family is located in 3-13, near Richard Cogdell.

INTERESTING FACT:

The Bitting family is also related to the Israel family, by marriage.

Sheriff Rufus Cone had four children who died between 1897 and 1908. All four are buried at Highland.

1898 Judge William Todd Jewett died. He was the father of Albert Jewett, who farmed the family land near what is now Valley Center. William is located with wife Hetty (who died in 1877) and several of his children in 2-60.

William's father was Barzilla, who is buried in Illinois. William's son, city attorney E. B. Jewett is located at Maple Grove Cemetery.

March 6, 1899 Rev. Charles W. (Von) Buechel died. He was one of the founders of the German Methodist Church, which became Calvary Methodist. He was also Jim Guy's great grandfather. He is located in 1-222.

1899 The year after former Mayor John B. Carey's death, the Carey Hotel became known as the Eaton Hotel, after the new owner Ben Eaton.[89] John's grandson by the same name is buried at Highland, in 3-50-12A.

Prohibitionist Carry A. Nation smashed John Noble's painting at the Eaton, on Dec 27, 1900. Noble is located in 1-148, near his idol William "Buffalo Bill" Mathewson.

---

[89] Ben Eaton is interred in the mausoleum.

The front has a brass plaque. The back is engraved, but it is very hard to read.

September 27, 1899 "Father of Wichita," William "Dutch Bill" Greiffenstein died. Greiffenstein (pronounced *Gry-fen-stine)* was born in Germany on July 28, 1829 and originally came to the area in 1868, operating his first trading post at what is now Eberly Farms. He bought Durfee's Trading Post in 1871 with the money he won in a court case against General Sheridan, for being unfairly kicked out of the area. "Dutch Bill" (and sometimes also known as "Uncle Billy") was later the 5th and then 7th Mayor of Wichita.

William and Catherine left Wichita in 1892, after the 'bust' of 1889.

Catherine Burnet's father was Chief Abram Burnet. The city of Burnet, OK is named for him. It was founded on the land she had been allotted because of her Potawatami heritage, and where William and Catherine both died. Both were brought back to Wichita for burial and are located in 1-54.

INTERESTING FACTs:

Dutch Bill should actually be spelled "Deutsch Bill", which literally means German Bill.

Greiffenstein's first wife was known as Cheyenne Jenny. She was killed in 1868 trying to protect Bill in an indian attack.

His second wife, Catherine was one of the first Catholics in Wichita., the religion of her mother.

October 5, 1900 John Davidson, Sr. died. A native of Scotland, Davidson was a 19-year resident of Wichita. Sons John, Jr. and William, and wife Agnes are located in 1-8.

June 9, 1901 *Wichita Eagle* article. Woodmen of the World parade to Highland to dedicate the monument of the first member of the Order to die in Wichita, Jasper E. Oder. He is located in 4-368-2. (There is a simple, ground level marker there for Mr. Oder, now.)

1902 Early homesteader and one of the founders of the First Presbyterian Church, Robert S. Cook died. He is located in 3-96-10.[90]

His casket cost $75.00, embalming (not a common practice) was $25.00 and Gill Mortuary's cost was $113.00 for the service.

March 10, 1902 Peter Getto died. He sold real estate, and his building at 2nd and Main was used for Christian Science services. He is located in 1-44-1.

1902 New First Presbyterian Church building started on Lawrence St. (now, Broadway) Street. The building was completed in 1912.

August 19, 1903 Joseph P. Allen died. He was the first druggist and Wichita's 9th mayor. His administration was known as the "sewer administration" because of changes he tried to make in the infrastructure of Wichita for the health of his constituents.[91] He is located in 1-2-5.

Oct 31, 1903 Mollie Walker, African American wife of Joshua and mother of Richard, died. She is located in 4-266-4.[92]

---

[90] Robert S. Cook's biography is in Chapman, 1888. Page 1003.
[91] Sedgwick County Medical Society book, p. 29
[92] Colored Citizen, October 30, 1902, page 3.

1903 Peter Coggeshall died. He is located in 1-18. Daughter Susie married W. S. Rogers, photographer.

1906 William H. Sternberg, architect died. He is located in 4-28-10.

INTERESTING FACT:

Durfee Ranch was located where the W. H. Sternberg mansion is now.

The Sternberg Mansion is located at 1065 N. Waco and is on the National Registry.

1904 James Baldock died. He is located in 3-117 next to his family under a grouping of ornamental trees.

1906 Roland P. Murdock died. He was the brother of Marshall, the business manager of *The Wichita Eagle* and the husband of Louise Caldwell Murdock. He is located in 3-79-11.

1906 Hooper G. Toler, father of Sidney Toler, equine breeder and owner of the Toler Opera House, died of Bright's Disease. He is located next to his mother Susan and family, in 4-145.

1907 Daniel Shelby Wilson died. He was a Civil War Union veteran and is located next to his family in 3-192.

1907 Benajah Aldrich, early Wichita druggist and 8th Mayor died. He is located in 2-14-3.

When a stone appears unfinished, it symbolizes an unfinished life.

1907 Enoch Dodge died. In 1869, he and his brothers A. E. and Frank settled in what first known as Elgin, then West Wichita, and finally Delano. His home was at 1406 W. 2nd, which is now on the National Register. He is located at 4-216-3.

1907 Fritz Schnitzler died. Born in Germany in 1835, he arrived in Wichita in 1877. His saloon, which was originally located at 112 E Douglas, has been rebuilt at Cowtown and the picture on the front of the building is of him. Fritz was on the City Council 1889-91.

His son Henry ran an establishment at 117 N. Market, in 1885.

Fritz is located in 2-242 and Henry is located in 2-243. Grandson, Henry Jr. is in the mausoleum.

Jan 2, 1908 Marshall Murdock died of liver and stomach ailments. Moved from a plot in 3-107 to Old Mission Mausoleum on December 8, 1930, with wife Victoria and daughter Lov' N Tangle. They were moved to Old Mission when the third section of the mausoleum was completed.

Highland was segregated at one time, as evidenced by this excerpt from an article about the burial of Ida Herman, born May 30, 1908, died June 8, 1908, and buried June 9, 1908.

"When the sexton found that it was a colored body he informed the grief-stricken father that the colored child could not be buried in the already dug grave and the parents had to remain in their hacks while another grave was dug in another part of the cemetery." [93]

Her sister Nadine, born March 15 and died March 23, 1907, is also buried next her, in 4-265-21.

---

[93] "Color Line in Cemetery" Wichita Searchlight newspaper (June 13, 1908), p 5; Ida's obituary, page 2.

Was the sexton in the article John Royal, or was it Mr. Rochelle? Or was it someone at Maple Grove? We may never really know.

INTERESTING FACT:

Farley A. Gackenbach is described in O. H. Bentley's 1910 book as having "the credit of the establishing separate schools in Wichita." [94] Gackenbach was on the school board from 1906-08 and the school board president until 1909, the same year that the Wichita schools were legally segregated.

1908 Katherine Masterson, mother of Bartholomew "Bat" Masterson died of apoplexy. Thomas and Katherine lived in Sunnydale with their children. The homestead was on 93rd Street, between what is now Oliver and Woodlawn. The family (except for Bat) is located in 2-70.[95]

March 30, 1908 Dr. Edwin Bird Allen died. Dr. Allen signed the city charter, was the coroner from 1870-75, was the first mayor of Wichita, and on the first school board. He also served in the Kansas House of Representatives three times.[96]

He is located at 3-85-11, next to his wife Mary.

---

[94] Bentley, 1910, p 774-775.
[95] 1882 City map; Masterson book; Andreas; 1885 1885 Census; 1900 Census
[96] A History of the Sedgwick County Medical Society- Dr. Howard C. Clark; p. 15, 22-23.

E. B. Allen's family marker

1908 Ellen Boggs died in Oklahoma. She is located in 2-182-11, next to her husband Wilberforce and one of their sons, Paul.[97]

---

[97] First Presbyterian Church history book.

1909 Alice Shinn died. She and her family are located in 1-116. Their stones were completely covered by grass until 2017, when we uncovered them.

1910 Gov. William E. Stanley died. He was a member of the First Presbyterian Church, former Sedgwick County Attorney, Wichita School Board member and the second Governor from Wichita--the 15th Governor of Kansas 1899-1903. He and his family are located in 3-168.

INTERESTING FACT:

Martin Eby's wife Melodee is the great granddaughter of Governor Stanley. Her father was Laurence Stanley, the son of Harry and grandson of William.[98]

1910 Hannah Lewellen Ward died. She married John Ward in 1870, and they were known as the "Honeymoon Couple" upon which the "story and a half house" at Cowtown is based. They were divorced on June 17, 1895. Hannah is located in 3-142 with the Ward family. John is buried in Illinois with his second wife.

Hannah's daughter Henrietta Ward Widdows is located in 3-151-7, and Henrietta's daughter, May E. Widdows Mason, is located in 3-151-6.

---

[98] Also, see 1953 and 1975 Eagle articles about Harry Stanley's leadership of Highland.

November 23, 1910 Lizzie Green died. Mother of Mrs. W. E. Whitted. She is located in 4-258-8.

1910 First Presbyterian Church brick church sold, and Grace Presbyterian Church started. A.A. Hyde was one of the two founders, using half of the money from the sale to start a church on the east side.[99]

1911 Vital statistics and death certificates required to be kept at Topeka.[100]

1911 Emmitt Slyter was struck by a Rock Island Engine and killed. He was Doc and Susanah's Lewellen's grandson, by his daughter Emma Lewellen Slyter's daughter Elmina Stice. Emmitt's family (Lewellens, Slyters and Stices) is also nearby, in 1-42.

June 19, 1912 Sidney S. Summers died. He was a confederate naval officer on the CSS Indian Chief. His son Birtie's marker was one that was recovered in 2012 from Haysville and has been replaced. They are located in 1-115.

1912 William Waldo Haines died. Haines was the first municipal police chief, in 1887. That position later became known as the Wichita Police Department's Police Chief. He is located in 4-253-3.

[99] First Presbyterian Church history book.
[100] Sedgwick County's Genealogy brochure, 2012.

1913 Samuel H. Hoover died. His land at Central and West was known as Hoover Orchard. He is located with family in 1-6.[101]

1914-18 World War I. United States involvement was 1917-1918.

1914 Richard Dodds, Civil War veteran and Wichita Grocer, died. He is located in 1-118.

---

[101] Westside Story, p. 56.

November 27, 1914 Christian Kimmerle died. He was a local monument maker, and it was said that he had the most expensive gravestone at Highland, at the time of his death.

July 8, 1889 Block 2, plot 19 sold to Christian Kimmerle for $65.00.

December 13, 1914 *Beacon* Article about the death of Victoria Murdock. In 1930 she was moved to Old Mission Mausoleum. [102]

April 26, 1915 Louise Caldwell Murdock died. Wife of Roland P. Murdock, her endowment started the Wichita Art Museum in 1935. The Carnegie Library, which she helped design, was completed just after her death. She is located at 3-79-10 next to her husband.

---

[102] Wichita Beacon, December 13, 1914

January 16, 1916 James Oakley Davidson died. He was married twice. First to Ida and then to Bessie. He started many ventures such as the Riverside Land Co, Burton Car Works, Wichita Watch Factory, Wichita Street Railway and was president of Citizen's Bank. He built Kirby Castle in 1888. His brother was Charles Lock Davidson, himself a mayor, who is interred at the mausoleum. James is buried in 3-86-6, next to both wives.

December 1916 Arthur Sim, son of Riverside land owner Coler Sim, was murdered in Kansas City. The land in Riverside was donated to the city (L. W. Clapp, Mayor) and named Sim park after Arthur by his father Coler Sim. The family is located in 3-172.[103]

March 21, 1916 City founder, best friend of W. C. Woodman, savior of 2-year old Hanna Rea Woodman in 1872, and "Four Horsemen" member **William "Buffalo Bill" Mathewson** died.

He died the same year as his third wife, Olive. (First wife Elizabeth Inman, whom he married in 1864 died in 1885. Second wife Carolyn Tarlton, whom he married in 1886, died in 1909.) Williams's service cost $666.00. William is located in 1-161-12, next to all three wives.

INTERESTING FACT:

Kiowa Indian chief Satanta nick-named Bill "sinpah zilbah" for "long bearded dangerous white man" after a fight between the two, after Bill caught Satanta from trying to steal from his trading post. They became friends after that!

Lizzie's indian name was "marr wissi" for "golden hair".

---

[103] Wichita Eagle, December 19, 1916. Several subsequent articles were written about his murder trial.

William "Buffalo Bill" Mathewson and his three wives.

1916 Alice Billadeau Rogers (Irwin), aka "The Nightingale" died. Born in Philadelphia, she had been a high society singer in New York. However, after her first husband George Billadeau died, she was swindled out of her insurance settlement by her second husband, Harry Rogers. She soon became an alcoholic, spending several days in jail sobering up, which is where she earned her nickname. Harry G. Irwin was the name of the barkeep she worked for at 515 E William. She is located in 2-126-10 next to George Billadeau.

1916 Frank Dyer was the Wichita School Supt 1895-1901 and State Assistant Superintendent of Instruction in 1903. He died in 1916 and is located in 2-27-12.

1917 Thomas Downin died. He was related to the Israel family. The Downins are located in 3-269 and 2R-239.

1918 National influenza epidemic. There was an obvious spike in the number of burials at Highland as well (393 that year.) The average burials per year is 118, in the 144 years of records at Highland.

1918 College Hill Cemetery (which changed its name to White Chapel Cemetery in 1922) founded.[104]

> *A White Chapel contract from 1954 shows that non-caucasians were not be buried next to caucasians. In other words, White Chapel was segregated by contract.*

1918 Jacob McAfee died. A Civil War Union veteran, Jacob was one of the first two African American settlers in Wichita. He is located in 3-372.

Jacob is the father of Abraham, a Spanish American War veteran. Abraham was also a homesteader in Garden Plain in the 1880s and died in 1929. Abraham is located in 4-109-9. Abraham's son was Arthur (located at Old Mission) and Arthur's son is architect Charles McAfee.

---

[104] Wichita Beacon, November 19, 1918.

1918 Charles M. Garrison died. His wife was Sarah Grantham Garrison, sister of Mary J. Allen, the wife of Dr. Edwin B Allen. Located in 1-103; and of Mary Sweeney, located in 2-119.

1918 Catherine Greiffenstein wife of William "Dutch Bill" Greiffenstein died.

Her service cost $78.00, which included shipping her body back here from the city she founded in Oklahoma. She is located in 1-54-4 next to her husband and son.

1918 Old Mission Mausoleum founded. There were six units built, between 1918 and 1954. George A. Saxton was the builder and three architects are credited with its design. George Siedhoff was the contractor.[105]

February 2, 1918 *Vidette* and *Beacon* editor Fred A. Sowers died. He founded *The Wichita Vidette, The Beacon*, was the second county clerk, was on the cemetery board and sold real estate. He is in 1-52-1. Wife Mary is located in 1-52-9.

1919 Old Mission Cemetery founded.

1919 *Negro Star* was relocated to Wichita and ran until 1953 when founder. Rev. Hallie (Hollie) T. Sims died. Rev. Sims also founded the local NAACP chapter. His wife Virginia died 1989, at age 103. He is located in 5-45-1 and she is located in 5-45-7.

---

[105] Wichita Daily Eagle, coupon (order form) on October 26, 1919.

Front.

Back.

October 27, 1919 Mrs. George B. Stearns died. Her marker is the one that we dug up from underground with a planter on top of it. She is located in 1-200-2.

The front of the marker says:

B. July ___, 185____

D. Oct. 26, 1919

Before.   After.

1919 Katie Lunnam died. Cheryl Wilson's family (the Fooshee family.) She is located in 4-150-9.

1920 Cpl. Samuel Smith died. He was a solider in Co. K of the 117th United States Colored Infantry (Union). He is located in 3-344-3.

December 1920 Sarah Krumm, mother of first child born in Sedgwick County (Sedgwick Hoover, b. 1869) died. She is located in 3-291-7.[106]

1920 George Lee Pratt died. He is located in 3-98.

---

[106] Wichita Eagle, December 19, 1920

1920 Sarah and George Davidson and George McKay all died. They are all family of Jovonne Jones and are all located in 3-307.

1921 Measles outbreak.

July 9, 1921 Eli Carter died, and he is located in block 5. Services held by Anderson Undertaker (An early African American mortuary in Wichita.)[107]

1921 Thomas Masterson, Sr. died of cardiac arrest. Thomas (1827-1921) and Katherine (1832-1908) lived in Sunnydale with their children. (Bat died in New York City.) Nine members of their family are buried in 2-70.

Daughter Nellie was married to James Cairns, who had been hired at the same time as Wyatt Earp and was later a sheriff.[108]

July 1921 Five-year old child Raymond Brown died and is buried in block 5. An African American, Anderson Undertaker held the service.[109]

1921 Dorothy Sims Winston (first African American graduate of WSU) opens a school of music. She was Gloria Sims McAfee's Aunt. Hollie Sims' sister (publisher of the *Negro Star*.)

November 1921 Death of gangster and career criminal Eddie Adams. His body was kept in cold storage at Highland until KU received permission to have his body for medical research, in February of 1922. Therefore, he was not buried anywhere.

---

[107] Negro Star, July 9, 1921
[108] Masterson book, Denver Public Library; Andreas, 1888; 1900 Census.
[109] Negro Star, July 2, 1921

1922 Ella Stocker died. She and husband Allen are located in 3-355-11.

And, coincidently:

1922 Wilber Warne died. He and his family are in 3-355 and in 2R-206.

September 1922 Clara Dawson Fountain died. (aged 121 years?) She is located in 4-262-5.

The article says she had been born in Culpepper County, VA in 1801, but would President George Washington have been in his second term? She remembered the war of 1812, the Indian wars, the Mexican war of 1849 and the civil war. She said her mother was a slave and her father was a white man. She married a slave, Andrew Gath at age 15. Then married Nelson Briley, and then married a 'Fountain'. She said she was 58 at the time of the Civil War. Two sons in the war, one was a spy. She lived in Charleston, SC and Louisville, KY. She also moved to Hastings, NE and then Wichita. It was when she was in Hastings, that descendants of her former master sent her records that proved her birth. One son, aged 72 Dawson Briley and 12 grandchildren. Her service was at Mathews Methodist Episcopal Church.[110]

1922 Lewis Sovereign died two weeks before his wife, Mary. They are located in 4-113-9 next to their daughter, Effie.

---

[110] *Topeka Plaindealer*, September 15, 1922.

1922 Easther King died. We found her (and her husband's) wooden markers in block 3 while working on another marker, nearby. The Kings are located in 3-246-1.

June 13, 1923 Coler Sim died. He owned Riverside Park after taking it over from the Keene Syndicate, who took it over from J. O. Davidson. Sim Park is named for his son, Arthur who was killed in 1916. He is located in 3-172-10.

1923 Mary Elizabeth Myers Carey[111], second wife of former Mayor John B. Carey, died. She and her family are located in 2-29.

Her son Charles' son, also named John B. Carey, is located in 3-50-12A.

Mayor John B. Carey (1828-1899) died in San Jose, CA and is buried at Texas Cemetery, in Clinton, ILL near his first wife, Sarah.

---

[111] Cutler refers to her as Mary A. Myers Carey.

1923 African American businessman Rev. John Henry Van Leu died. Van Leu was a very successful real estate developer in Sedgwick County and missionary for the Kansas Baptist Convention. His son Wendell was the first black student to graduate from Friends, in 1926.[112]

He is buried in 3-367 with his wife Julia and near six of his 13 children, which is at the north side of the block near Jacob McAfee and many other African Americans from the time.

1923 Clara B. Caldwell Smith and her sister Mary Amanda Caldwell Lamb died in a car accident in Sterling.[113] Clara is located with her husband in 3-357. (Mary is buried in Sterling.)

1924 John Bottenberg died. He is buried in 1-237 with wife Mettie, under an ornate tree.

[112] TKAAM African Americans in Wichita history book
[113] Wichita Eagle, November 1923; Sterling paper, November 1923.

1924 Ed D. Shutz, aka "Crazy Ed" the junkman died. A poor man who had been bullied by neighborhood kids who was given a new stone by one of those kids after they had grown up. He is located in 1-287.[114]

Original marker. His name was spelled incorrectly.

New marker, with his name spelled correctly.

1924 James L. Dyer, first City Court judge died. He is located in 3-77-12.

1925 James Tipps, aka James Boyd, died.

[114] Tanner; and First Presbyterian Church tour notes.

He was an ex-slave. Boyd was his master's name, and Tipps was his father's name. There has been some argument about his military stone, and which side he really fought for in the Civil War. He was either in the KY or VA military. What we do know is he did own a downtown laundry.

He is located in 3-269-6A.

1925 William Fike died. He is located in 3-364-11.

The letters on these markers are formed by marbles, just as the road markers in downtown Wichita were at the turn of the century.

1926 Richard Cogdell died. Cogdell was a Confederate officer from Georgia in the Civil War (with Richard Tarlton) and elected the Sedgwick County Sherriff in 1877. He is located in 3-29-3.

1926 Phillip Paulus committed suicide in Riverside Park. He was the artist of the sculpture 'Buttermilk Lions' (1917) that is currently found outside Attorney Roger Riedmiller's office on Broadway. Paulus is located in 1-339-7.

INTERESTING FACT:

The sculptures are made using a mix of buttermilk, Portland concrete, granite dust and green marble that is known only to him.

January 27, 1926 This was the date of the first services held in Highland by Jackson Mortuary. It was for Vera May Cox, in 4-273-33.

INTERESTING FACT:

Jackson Mortuary was first located at 628 N. Main (1926). They then moved to 703 N. Water (1933), and finally moved to 1125 E. 13th in 1966 where they are currently located. An addition was made to the building in 1985 by Charles McAfee.

1928 Samuel L. Davis died. He is next to his wife, in 1-210.

1928 Martin Luther Garver died. He was the elder who with A. A. Hyde started the Grace Presbyterian Church. Garver's wife Kate started the Wichita Children's Home. They are located in 1-269-3.[115]

1929 Judge William C. Little died. He was also an investment banker and built the Boston Store building at the SE corner of Main and Douglas. He is interred in the mausoleum, B-3.

December 1930 Marshall Murdock and his family were reinterred to Old Mission Mausoleum, when the third section of that mausoleum was completed.[116]

1930 Joseph Wilbur Warne died. His wife Fern, son Wilbur and mother Louisa are next to him in 3-355. He also has family in 2R-206.

1931 Kos Harris died. Kosciuszko Kossuth Harris[117] came to Wichita from Iowa. He retired from law in 1924, 50 years to the day after he began. His son Vermillion took over the practice. Involved in the formation of the city of Maize (1886), and the Forum, BOE member 1881-85, and historian often quoted in Bentley's 1910 book. He was also an avid Greiffenstein supporter. Burial cost $475.00. Located in 2-164 with his parents, wife Ida and daughter Nourma. Vermillion is located at Maple Grove.

1933 Finlay Ross died. His first wife was Sallie Parham, and they had one daughter, Sara, together. Sara married the eldest son of Judge William Little.

After Sallie's death, Finlay married Ella Fuller, granddaughter of Nathaniel English. They had one daughter, Christina.

---

[115] Wichita Eagle, December 1, 1987
[116] Email from John Rodda
[117] His full name was confirmed by census records.

Furniture store owner, and the 13th and 15th Mayor, Ross donated a well-known statue, "Boy With Boot" to the city in lieu of a raise or bonus. The statue became part of the new park system, until it was destroyed in a car accident in Riverside Park. A cast of the original is now located at the Wichita Sedgwick County Historical Museum.

Mr. Ross is located in 4-32-9 with both the Ross and Parham families. His furniture store has been recreated at Cowtown.

1934 Former Mayor Lewis William Clapp died. He is located in the mausoleum.

July 10, 1934 Alfred Bitting died. He and his brother Charles founded the Bitting building. Except for Charles, the family is located in 3-13. Charles is interred at the Old Mission Mausoleum.

1934 Henry Schnitzler, Sr. died. He is located in 2-243.

January 6, 1934 John Noble, Jr. died of an overdose of medication, in NYC. He was the artist of "Cleopatra in her Bath", which was destroyed by Carry A. Nation on Dec 27, 1900. John lived in France for several years, and greatly admired Buffalo Bill Mathewson. So much so that he called himself "Wichita Bill" Noble. Irving Stone wrote a novel about Noble in 1949, "The Passionate Journey". He is located in 1-148-3, next to his idol, William "Buffalo Bill" Mathewson. His family is buried in New York and Maple Grove Cemetery.

1935 Maybelle Reynolds, great grandmother of Jackie Lugrand died. Service cost $25.00. She is buried in block 4.

1936 Dr. Frank O. Miller died. Dr. Miller became an OB/GYN in 1908, one of the first African American doctors in Wichita. His burial cost $25.00. He is located in 4-109-5. [118]

1937 Quiring Monument started. Funeral home built in 1940. Warehouse built in 1971. The building on 9th and North Hillside was demolished in 2017.

1942 William C. Hoover died. He was the son of Samuel Henry Hoover, Sr. (who died in 1913). William and his brother Edwin (who died in 1966) ran Hoover Orchards on land purchased by Samuel in 1882. The family is located in 1-6.[119]

October 3, 1943 Harry Theodore Bentley died. His anvil marker was returned to his gravesite in 2017 by us. He is located near his mother Mary in 4-157-1A.

---

[118] Who's Who of the Colored Race, 1915, page 192.
[119] Westside Story, p. 56.

His name is stamped in the metal near the top of the anvil, facing the east side. He was a metal worker, hence the anvil shape.

His mother is buried in the same plot.

1944 Eunice Sterling Unit of the Daughters of the American Revolution bought the Munger house. (It was donated to Historic Wichita, Inc. in 1952.)

October 21, 1944 John J. Jones, builder of the Jones 6 automobile died. Located in 1-245-1.

February 12, 1947 Sidney Toler died. His grandmother, father, brother and sister in law and their son are also buried at Highland. Sidney was better known to the world in the 1940s as "Charlie Chan." He is located in 4-145-10.

INTERESTING FACT:

His father had an equine farm NE of Wichita, and owned the Toler Opera House, which was where Sidney honed his craft from 1900-1912.

1947 Georgia Claypoole Swigert died. She was the first wife of William, a member of the Daughters of the American Revolution, and the Union Station Matron. Her two sons, Ray and Elza died in motorcycle accidents within a month of each other in 1914 and are buried next to her in 2-117.

1950 Formation of Historic Wichita, Inc., who then founded and operated Cow Town.

1951 Maple Grove office built.

1952 Fred Hummelke, Sr. died. His wife Lydia Anna Haines Hummelke was the daughter of William Waldo Haines. They are buried in 1-135. Her three brothers (including Edward, who was on the fire department) are buried at Highland as well.

1958 Resthaven Gardens of Memory founded by Hap Bledsoe. Name was changed to Resthaven Mortuary in 1970.

> *Carl Koster said Hap used to say "Cemeteries were the only land you could buy by the acre and sell by the foot."*

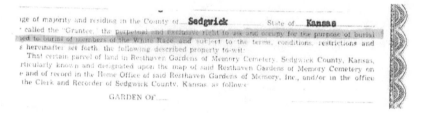

1959 Resthaven's contract showed that a caucasian and non-caucasian could not be buried next to one another. This was the case until 1964.

1963 Wendell Wallace Tyson died. He is located in Potters Field-2-6A.

1963 John B. Carey, grandson of Mayor John B. Carey died. He is located in 3-50-12A. His father Charles is located in 2-29-10.

June 1964 Baby girl Morland died. She is buried in an unmarked grave in 5-10-11.

July 1964 Civil Rights Act signed by President Lyndon B. Johnson. The law out laws discrimination based on race, color, religion sex or national origin in **public places** or in employment.

Jan 16, 1965 Piatt Street Crash, in which 30 died. Nine of those people are buried at Highland.[120]

Denise Jackson	5-35-4
Albert, Leslie, Wilma Bolden	5-35-2 and 3
Brenda Dunn	5-35-5
Emmitt Warmsley Sr and Jr	5-8-11 and 12
Laverne Warmsley and unborn child	Unmarked.

Final settlements for the crash were made in 1967.

1966 Bessie Carver Davidson, first wife of James Oakley Davidson, died. She was the mother of James Ogden Davidson. Service cost: $1,493.00. She is located in 3-86-5.

INTERESTING FACT:

Her mother's maiden name was Woodman. She was the niece of Commodore W. C. Woodman. Sister of Ella Woodman, who was married to Rea's brother, W. S.

---

[120] *May Day Over Wichita;* D. W. Carter, 2013.

1968 William L Schultz, architect of Riverview Apts., died. He is located in 1-83-1.

1969 Hans Richert died. Born in 1944, he was a member of North High School's class of 1963. He is located with Johann (John), Magdalena, and Elli in 3-141.

1972 A. Price Woodard, Jr the first African American Mayor (1970) of Wichita, died. He had also been a City Commission member and 76th Mayor of Wichita. He is buried next to his father, attorney Ambrose P. Woodard, Sr. who died in 1962. Sr. is in 5-7-12; Jr. is in 5-36-11.

1977 James W. White died. He is located in Potter's Field: PF-10-8D. (His stone was repaired and straightened by FWP in 2018.)

1979 Emma Lou Thomas, biological mother of Bill Billingsley, died. She is located in 5-115-3.

1984 George Edmund White died. He is located in 3-205 with his family.

1986 Ralph Baum died. He was Baum Hamburger stand owner, and Janiece Baum Dixon's uncle. He and his wife are located in 1-237, under an ornate tree.

November 16, 1990 North American Graves Protection & Repatriation Act (NAGPRA) was enacted to require institutions such as museums to follow a prescribed process for transferring culturally affiliated human remains and associated funerary objects to lineal descendants and associated Indian tribes.[121]

Native American and homesteaders' burials were once made by the river. If you find any kind of burial, by Federal Law you must stop and the Mid-American All Indian Center (MAAIC) must be contacted to assure that the integrity of the grave is kept.

2002 Article about the life and death of Jack Ledford[122]

2010 Kansas stopped paying the $550 benefit for indigent burials.

2011 National Register of Historic Places application for Jackson Mortuary was approved.[123]

CHAPTER SIX:

[121] www.nps.gov/nagpra accessed June 27, 2018.
[122] Wichita Eagle, May 2, 2002
[123] Ibid, June 28, 2011

So, where are...?

Feldin Buckner. A freed slave from Missouri. After working for James R. Mead, he moved to Osage County, although he might be buried in MO.

Jesse Chisholm. Indian trader and trailblazer of the cattle trail that would later be known as the Chisholm Trail. Died in 1868 and is buried at Kingfisher, OK which was Indian Territory at the time.

Elias Durfee. Owner of Durfee Ranch, brother in law of C. H. Peck, and member of the First Presbyterian Church. He died in 1874 and is buried at Leavenworth.

Wyatt Earp. Lawman, died in 1929 and is buried in Los Angeles, CA.

William Finn. Teacher and first surveyor of Wichita, Finn died in 1929, and is buried in Sedgwick, KS.

Abner Jackson, Sr. Founder of Jackson Mortuary. He and his family are all buried at Old Mission. His papers are kept at Kansas University.

Sol H. Kohn. Vice President of the Wichita Savings Bank (1872), Chairman of the Board of County Commissioners (1873), and first Jewish mayor of Wichita (1879.) After resigning from his office, he moved back to New York City the same year, and he died in 1920.

Doctor Zeddock "Doc" Lewellen. Former city grocer. He is buried at Belle Vista Cemetery in El Dorado. Many members of his family are either at Chelsea Cemetery, Ridgeway Cemetery, or at Highland Cemetery in Wichita.

Chester I. Lewis. Attorney and NAACP activist, Lewis died in 1990 and was cremated. His papers are held at Kansas University.

"Rowdy" Joe Lowe. The saloon owner was killed by a police officer in 1899 and buried in Denver, CO.

Bartholomew "Bat" Masterson. Former lawman, he was a sports journalist at the time of his death in 1921 and is buried in New York City.

Hattie McDaniel. Oscar winning actress. She died in Hollywood in 1952. She is buried in a segregated cemetery. She also has a marker in an integrated cemetery in Hollywood, CA.

James R. Mead and his son Bunnie – Town founder J. R. died in 1910 and both are in a family mausoleum at Maple Grove. His first wife is now buried at Davenport, IA. His second wife, Lucy is at Highland. His third wife, Fern, remarried and is buried at Maple Grove with her second husband.

John Meagher. Fellow lawman and brother of Mike. He died in 1930 and is buried in South Dakota.

Ewing Moxley and Edmund Mosely. Both killed, one by Indians in the door of his cabin; one, crossing a river while stealing stock. Both burial places are unknown.

Duane Nelson. Dockum Drugstore sit-in member and black cowboy reenactor at Cowtown. Mr. Nelson died in 2015 and was cremated.

William Smith. The brother of Henry Smith, he was the Wichita City Marshal 1873 and Sheriff 1874-75. William died in 1908 and is buried at Galena, KS with his second family.

John Marion "Big Jim" Steele. Wichita founder and real estate mogul. Steele moved to Tacoma, WA in 1880 and died in 1896. He and his family are located in Tacoma

Hannah Rea Woodman – Hannah came to Wichita in 1870 with her father W. C. Woodman. She was kidnapped by Indians and quickly recovered in 1872. Ms. Woodman died in 1951. She, her father Commodore W. C. Woodman and their family are located at Maple Grove.

Another interesting skill that I learned: Dousing.

One thing I get asked a lot is if I know Vince Marshall, and have I ever seen him douse? The answer to both is yes. I will note here that I have seen it at work numerous times!

*And one last **INTERESTING FACT**:*

Did you know that people used to be able to buy gravestones for $20 from the Sears catalog??

TABLES

1. Race

2. Mayors

3. Law Enforcement

4. Examples of sale prices in 1884-1886.

5. Military symbology

6. Clubs mentioned in obituaries

7. Causes of death (examples)

8. Religion

9. Undertakers, Funeral Homes, and Morticiians.

10. Ambulance and hearss

TABLE 1:

RACE IN HIGHLAND

Ratio of Race in each block.

Block 1	# of AA burials:	6
	Ratio of Block:	.3%
	Ratio of Cemetery:	<1%
Block 2	# of AA burials:	33
	Ratio of Block:	2.5%
	Ratio of Cemetery:	<1%
Block 2R	187 of 340 burials are African American	
Block 3	# of AA burials:	279
	Ratio of block:	8.7%
	Ratio of Cemetery:	1.6%
Block 4	# of AA burials:	644
	Ratio of block:	15%
	Ratio of cemetery:	3.7%
Block 5	# of AA burials:	1,652
	Ratio fo block:	56%
	Ratio of cemetery:	9.6%

AA = African American

A word on race at Highland:

The racial divide at the cemetery is 85% white:15% minority, which has also historically been the trend in the City of Wichita. But my thought through this project was always: "segregation in Kansas? A free state?" So, in my study of Highland, I also got a better look at the history of segregation in Wichita.

This is what I found. While not by contract, burials of African Americans have historically been sectioned off into five areas of Highland:

- The middle of block four was for affluent blacks. The exception was Henry Van Leu, a rich real estate developer, who is in block three; and A Price Woodard Jr, first black mayor, who is in block five.
- The farthest north areas of block three and four were always for blacks and indigents.
- Potter's Field is the northernmost areas of the cemetery, past the north road.
- Block five was added in 1924 and burials in that block are at least 75% conventional African American burials. The rest are infants. The block has about 5% white conventional burials.[124]
- There is also an area behind the mausoleum, known as block 2R, as in replat of block two, that is largely African American. In other words, burials of the minorities have often been pushed to the outer limits of the cemetery.

---

[124] I use the term 'conventional' to mean their death was from natural causes, such as old age, disease, accidents or murder, as opposed to infant deaths. Infant burials are in a separate area of block 5.

TABLE 2:

MAYORS

There are nine former Mayors (who served eleven terms) at Highland.

	#	Name	Served:	Location:
A	#1	Edwin B Allen	1871-72	3-85-11
B	#2 and 4	John G Hope	1873-74	1-267-1
C	#5 & 7	William Greiffenstein	1878-84	1-54-5
D	#8	Benajah Aldrich	1885-86	2-14-3
E	#9	Joseph P. Allen	1887-88	1-2-5
F	#11	John B. Carey. (He is not at Highland, but his family is.)		
G	#13	Finlay Ross	1897-1900 and 1905-06	4-32-9

#17   Charles L Davidson   1909-10
       Maus. A-2W

#22   L.W. Clapp   1917-19
       Maus G-2S

#76   A Price Woodard, Jr 1970-71
       5-36-11

Photos of all of the City of Wichita Mayors are posted in the Wichita City Hall lobby.

TABLE 3:

LAW ENFORCEMENT

From: The Wichita and Sedgwick County Law Enforcement
History Books

Marshals:

Mike Meagher 1871-74 and 75-77. Located in 1-17-10.

William Smith. 1873 (Galena)

Richard Cogdell 1877-78. Located in 3-29-3.

Dan Parks 1878-79. Located in 1-108-3.

James Cairns 1879-80. First time it was an appointed instead of elected position. Located in 2-25-5.

City Marshal (Police Chief):

William W Haines 1887-88. Located in 4-253-3.

Louis Aspy 1889. Located in 1-170-9.

The title was officially changed to Police Chief on Sept 1, 1899

Sheriff:

Jack Ledford 1871. Located in 1-96-6.

William Smith. 1874-75. (Galena.)

William W. Hays 1886 and 1888. Located in 4-95-12.

Richard Cogdell 1907-11. Located in 3-29-3.

TABLE 4

From 1884-86, the *Wichita Beacon* published land sale records, which included sales of cemetery plots. The following is a selection of plots which were sold in those years and their prices:

Aug 31, 1884 Block 3, lot 63, sells to D. L. Miller for $18.00.

Sept 20, 1884, Block 1, lot 216 sells to C. R. Viney for $11.00.

Nov 6, 1884 Block 3-23 sells to W. B. Smith for $14.00.

July 14, 1885 Block 3, lot 86 sells to J. O. Davidson for $20.00

July 22, 1885 block 4, lot 109 (south quarter) sells to Thomas Glover
(AA) for $3.00. Block 4-109 was later sold to Sallie Rowles.

July 22, 1885 block 4, lot 391 (half) sold to Ed Langford
(AA) for $9.00.

Feb 16, 1886 Block 1, plot 83 (half) sold to Hallie Hain for $10.00.

March 6, 1886 Block 1, plot 73 (half) George Chadwick for $8.00.

April 11, 1886 Block 1 plot 261 sold to J. D. Hewitt for $30.00.

April 17, 1886 Block 1, plot 157 sold to E. P. Ford for $50.00.

June 26, 1886 sold back to the cemetery, for $10.00.

1886 Block 1, lot 128 (north quarter) sells to J. Love for $5.00.

June 26, 1886 block 1, plot 76 (quarter) sold to G. W. Salander
for $3.00.

July 20, 1886 Block 3, plot 54 sold to T. Tull for $12.00.

July 26, 1886 block 1, plot 42 sold to W. McCullock (Lewellen's)
for $12.50?

July 29, 1886 block 3, plot 27 sold to S. S. Riddle for $12.00.

August 5, 1886 block 4, plot 9 sold to Garrison for $45.00.

August 31, 1886 block 1, plot 206 sold to S. Whitehorn for $25.00.

August 31, 1886 block 4, plot 365 (half) sold to Millie Hodge
for $12.00.

TABLE 5

MILITARY SYMBOLOGY:

Military symbology:

Confederate and Union stones differ in one way: Shape. Confederate stones will have the same front, but an angular top.

Peter L. Coggeshall (1824-1903). Located in 1-18-2.

Military markers are installed by the Veteran's Administration. Markers are taken care of by the Sons of the Union Veterans Corp. Patrick Coyne Camp No. 1.

Coins left on gravestones are in recognition of deceased who had a military background.

> *Penny* – Shows that you were someone who did not know them well but shows that you visited.

> *Nickel* – Shows that you went through boot camp together.

> *Dime* – Shows that you served with the soldier in some capacity; or, you were a friend who served in another platoon in the same company.

> *Quarter* – Shows that you served in the same outfit, or that you were with the soldier when they were killed.

Half-dollars and gold-dollars are also left, sometimes to show a rank of officer. All coins at National cemeteries are collected and donated for the maintenance of the graves.

The local Veterans of Foreign Wars (VFW) Over There Post #112 has been putting up flags on Memorial Day since 1920.

Brass military flag holders remain at the cemetery, and denote which war or era they would have been in. Flag holders can be purchased by anyone, or from the Veteran's Administration.

TABLE 6

CLUBS MENTIONED IN OBITUARIES:

Clubs represented at Highland:

Woodmen of the World – Founded in 1890, members of this insurance fraternity received a gravestone as a part of their death benefits until the 1920s. Gravestones usually looked like a tree or pile of logs.

This is conveniently located next to a tree!

IOOF – International Order of Oddfellows, Lodge 93. The "poor man's free masons" was founded in 1819. The initials FLT stand for Friendship, Love, and Truth.

Other groups represented at Highland:

American Legion

Ancient Order of United Workmen, Lodge No. 22

Eastern Star (The female counterpart to the Free Masons.)

Eunice Sterling Chapter of the Daughters of the American Revolution

Free and Accepted Masons, Wichita Lodge 99, AF & AM

Grand Army of the Republic, Garfield Post No. 25

Knights of Columbus

Knights of Honor, Wichita Lodge 528

Knights of Pythias, No. 440

Knights of Templar, Lodge 45

Shriners

Wichita Chapter, No. 33

Wichita Lodge, No. 93

TABLE 7

CAUSES OF DEATH

Infant Mortality:

There were 1,654 babies buried in 100 years. Avg 16.5 per year. Compares to:

713 African American babies being buried at Highland, in a 40-year span (1926-66.) That is an average of 17.8 per year.

That is higher than average black infant mortality.

Causes of death in the early years of Highland Cemetery include:

Puerperal Fever (commonly known as 'in childbirth')

Yellow Fever

Scarlet Fever

Influenza

Diarrhea

Palsy

Bright's Disease

Murder, accidents, and unknown causes.

TABLE 8

RELIGION:

Jewish custom is to place a rock or item on a grave marker when you visit.

Different religious items have been left at Highland. This Bible was left in this location for six months!

TABLE 9

UNDERTAKERS, FUNERAL HOMES AND MORTICIANS

From: Midwest Historical and Genealogical Society

& Kansas Trails[125]

Mortuary: Formerly or also known as:	Opening year (if known):	
Advantage Funeral Services	2002	
*Anderson Undertaking	Before 1920	
All Faiths Mortuary		
Affinity		
Baker Funeral Home		
*Bethea's		
*Biglow Funeral Directors	2007	
Cochran	1928	
Cochran-Byrd		
Culbertson-Smith	1930	
Holmes Mortuary	1919	
Culbertson	1930	
Westside Undertaking	1918	(Run by Mr. Holmes)
Cozine Memorial Group	2008	
Broadway Mortuary	1938	
Kensington Gardens	1995	
Downing & Lahey Mortuary		
Crest-Hill		

---

[125] Wichita Daily Eagle, October 3, 1920.

Downing Mortuary

Lahey Mortuary

Lahey & Martin   1926

Grover

City Undertaking   1913 (Run by Mr. Lahey and Mr. Martin)

Wichita Undertaking   Before 1920

(Run by Mr. Butchart and Mr. Downing)

DeVorss, Flanagan-Hunt Mortuary

DeVorss Mortuary

Flanagan-Hunt Mortuary

Dignity

Dunbar   1882

Dunbar & Bleitz   1902

Bleitz & Burbank   1903

JJ Bleitz   1903

Flanagan & Bourman   Before 1920

Flanagan-Hunt

Gill Mortuary[126]

Figg & Boaz

Boaz & Gill   1889

IW Gill Mortuary   1891

Gill Mortuary   1921

Gordon Mortuary   1929

Hillside Funeral Home   1991

Byrd-Snodgrass   1938

---

[126] Isaac Wesley Gill's obituary was published in the Wichita Eagle, May 10, 1935, and gave a history of Gill Mortuary. The records for Gill are at the Wichita Public Library.

Byrd-Hillside	1938
Dignity	
*Jackson Mortuary	1926
Hiram W. Kendle, Undertaker	1875
Kendle & Holmes	
Holmes	1885
Kirker & Marsh	
Lakeview Funeral Home	1962
Dignity	
A. G. Mueller[127]	1889
Old Mission Funeral Home	1962
Quiring Mortuary	1911
Quality Funerals	
*People's Undertaking	Before 1920
Resthaven Mortuary	1959
Dignity	
Van Gettis Funeral Services	
*Citizen's Funeral Home	1953
*Vann Funeral service	
Watson Funeral Home	

*African American owned businesses.

---

[127] Records for Mueller Mortuary are at the Wichita Public Library.

TABLE 10

Ambulance services in 1920 were run by mortuaries:

City Undertaking, A G Mueller and Gill Brothers Mortuary were three of the companies which ran ambulances. Abner Jackson, Sr. drove an ambulance for another undertaker until 1926 when he began his own mortuary, for African Americans.

Gill Mortuary's original horse-drawn hearse, at Cowtown.

CEMETERY PLOT MAPS

Thank you to Bill Pennington for permission to use maps from ksgenweb.org.

Plots:

(NORTH)

7	6
8	5
9	4
10	3
11	2
12	1

Infant plots might actually have more than 12 burials.

The exception to the plot numbering system is Potter's Field.

Please see page 162 (Map 10) for a map.

Please also note that there are several sections of Potter's Field.

499 and 500 are attached to the south of Section 5,

501 and 502 are attached to the north of Section 4.

503 is attached to the west of Section 4.

MAP 1: HIGHLAND CEMETERY

Please use the QR code on page 11 for a full burial list.

NORTH

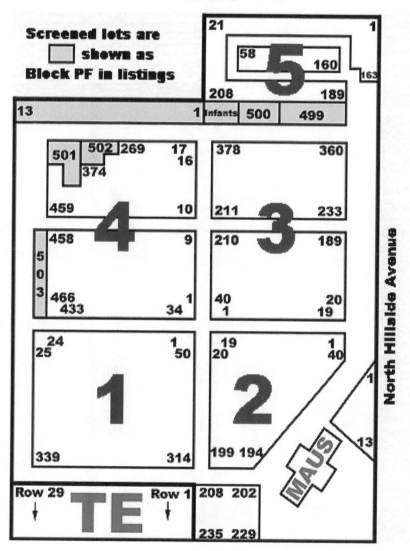

SOUTH

MAP 2:
TEMPLE EMANU-EL (TE)
JEWISH CEMETERY

EAST

WEST

MAP 3:

BLOCK 1

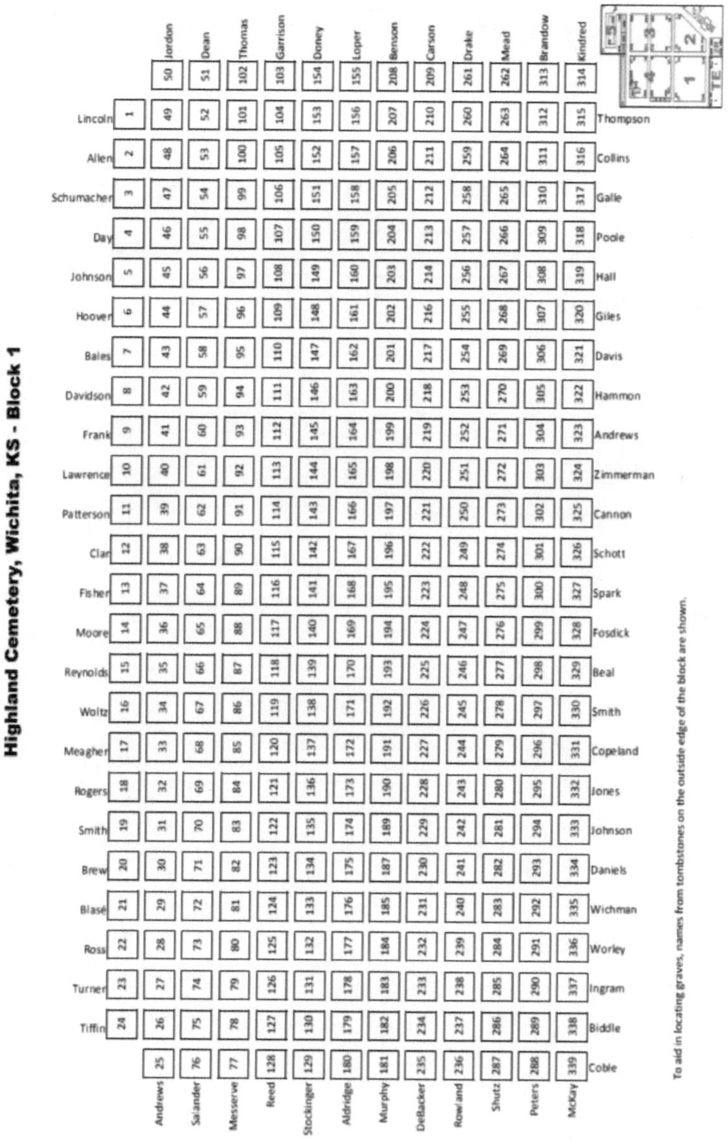

Highland Cemetery, Wichita, KS - Block 1

Top edge names (left to right): Jordon 50, Dean 51, Thomas 102, Garrison 103, Doney 154, Loper 155, Benson 208, Carson 209, Drake 261, Mead 262, Brandow 313, Kindred 314

Left edge names (top to bottom): Lincoln 1, Allen 2, Schumacher 3, Day 4, Johnson 5, Hoover 6, Bales 7, Davidson 8, Frank 9, Lawrence 10, Patterson 11, Clar 12, Fisher 13, Moore 14, Reynolds 15, Woltz 16, Meagher 17, Rogers 18, Smith 19, Brew 20, Blase 21, Ross 22, Turner 23, Tiffin 24

Right edge names (top to bottom): Thompson 315, Collins 316, Galle 317, Poole 318, Hall 319, Giles 320, Davis 321, Hammon 322, Andrews 323, Zimmerman 324, Cannon 325, Schott 326, Spark 327, Fosdick 328, Beal 329, Smith 330, Copeland 331, Jones 332, Johnson 333, Daniels 334, Wichman 335, Worley 336, Ingram 337, Biddle 338, Coble 339

Bottom edge names (left to right): Andrews 25, Salander 76, Messerve 77, Reed 128, Stockinger 129, Aldridge 180, Murphy 181, DeBacker 235, Rowland 236, Shutz 287, Peters 288, McKay 339

To aid in locating graves, names from tombstones on the outside edge of the block are shown.

160

MAP 4:

BLOCK 2

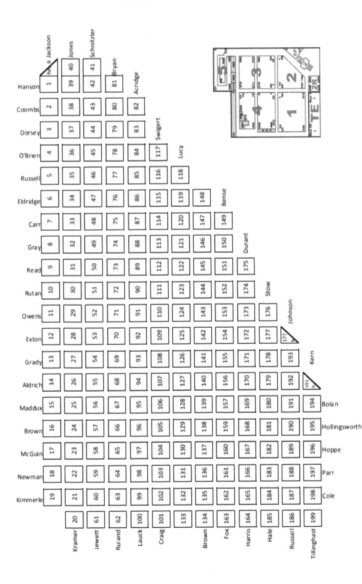

Highland Cemetery, Wichita, KS - Block 2

To aid in locating graves, names from tombstones on the outside edge of the block are shown.

MAP 5

BLOCK 2R:

EAST

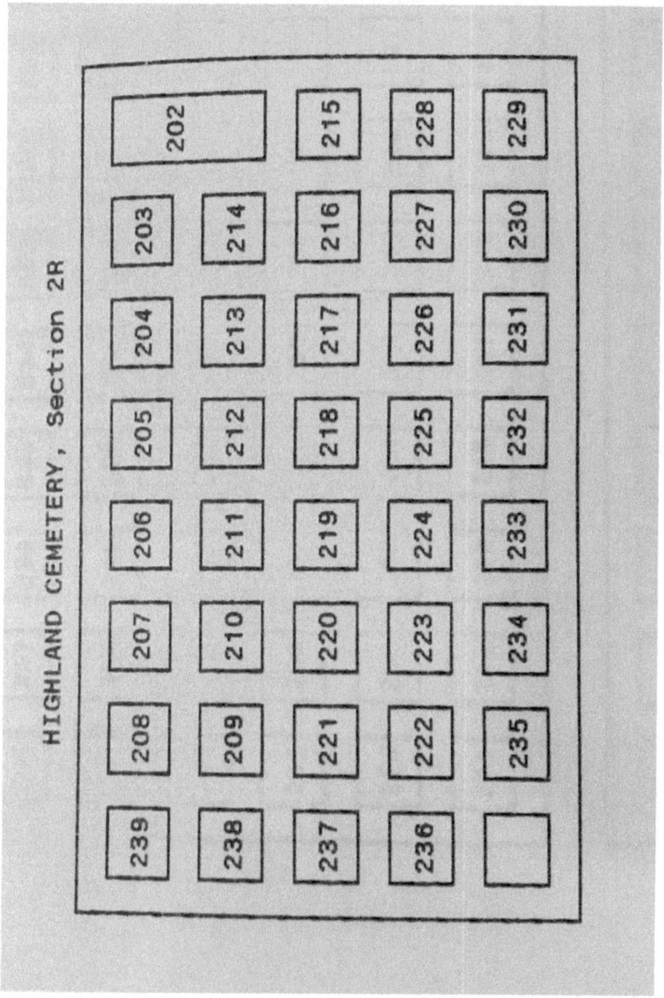

HIGHLAND CEMETERY, Section 2R

202	215	228	229
203	214	216	227	230
204	213	217	226	231
205	212	218	225	232
206	211	219	224	233
207	210	220	223	234
208	209	221	222	235
239	238	237	236	

MAP 6:

BLOCK 3

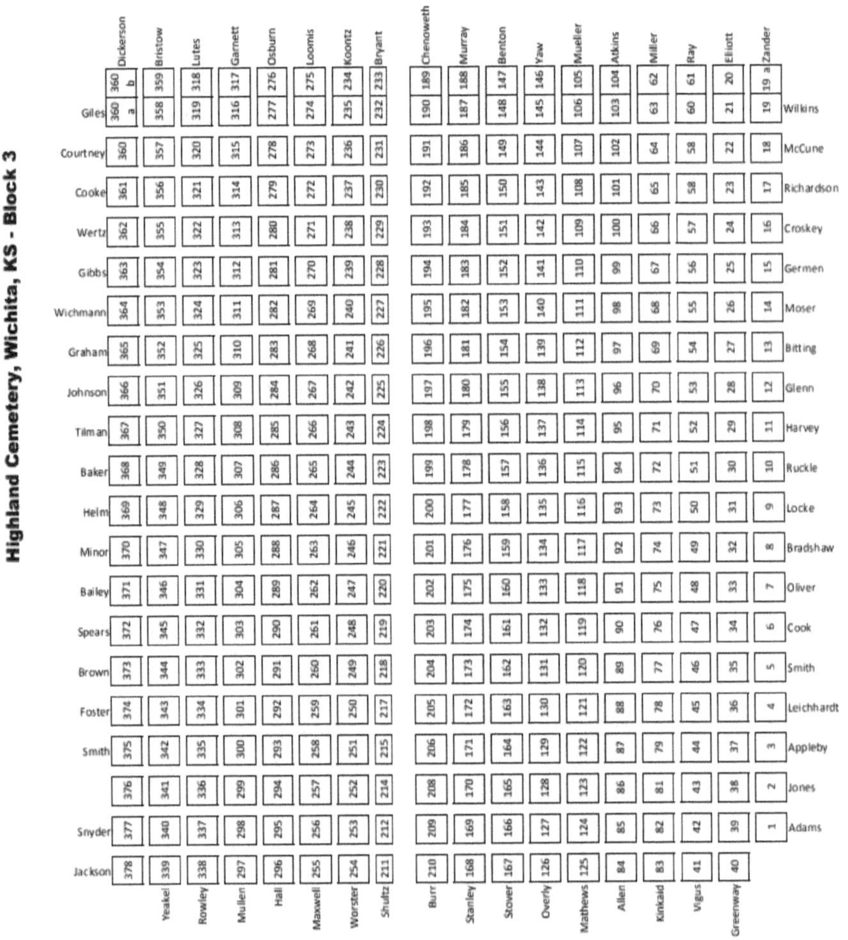

Highland Cemetery, Wichita, KS - Block 3

To aid in locating graves, names from tombstones on the outside edge of the block are shown.

MAP 7:

BLOCK 4

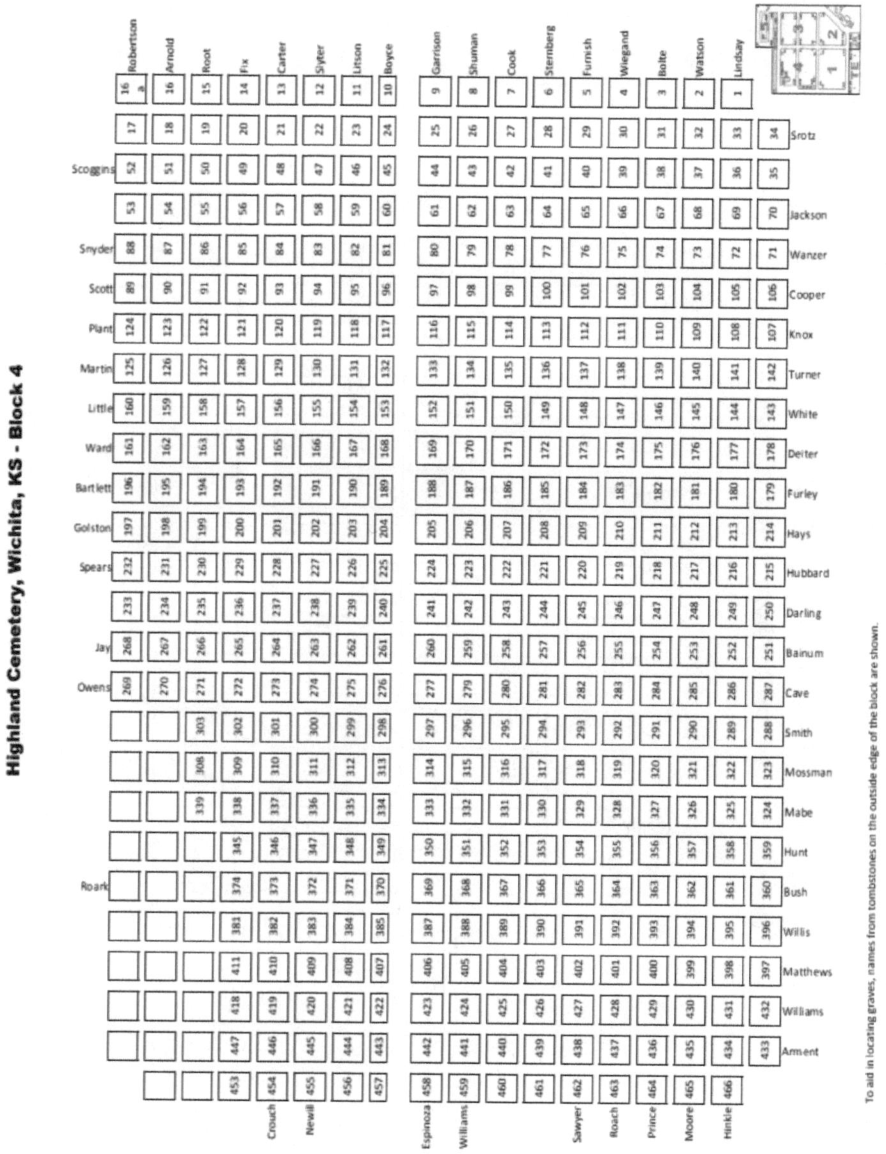

Highland Cemetery, Wichita, KS - Block 4

Column labels (top, left to right): Robertson, Arnold, Root, Fix, Carter, Slyter, Litson, Boyce, Garrison, Shuman, Cook, Sternberg, Furnish, Wiegand, Bolte, Watson, Lindsay

Right-side row labels (top to bottom): Srotz, Jackson, Wanzer, Cooper, Knox, Turner, White, Deiter, Furley, Hays, Hubbard, Darling, Bainum, Cave, Smith, Mossman, Mabe, Hunt, Bush, Willis, Matthews, Williams, Arment

Left-side row labels: Scoggins, Snyder, Scott, Plant, Martin, Little, Ward, Bartlett, Golston, Spears, Jay, Owens, Roark

Bottom labels (left group): Crouch, Newell; (right group): Espinoza, Williams, Sawyer, Roach, Prince, Moore, Hinkle

Robertson	Arnold	Root	Fix	Carter	Slyter	Litson	Boyce		Garrison	Shuman	Cook	Sternberg	Furnish	Wiegand	Bolte	Watson	Lindsay
16a	16	15	14	13	12	11	10		9	8	7	6	5	4	3	2	1
17	18	19	20	21	22	23	24		25	26	27	28	29	30	31	32	33	34
52	51	50	49	48	47	46	45		44	43	42	41	40	39	38	37	36	35
53	54	55	56	57	58	59	60		61	62	63	64	65	66	67	68	69	70
88	87	86	85	84	83	82	81		80	79	78	77	76	75	74	73	72	71
89	90	91	92	93	94	95	96		97	98	99	100	101	102	103	104	105	106
124	123	122	121	120	119	118	117		116	115	114	113	112	111	110	109	108	107
125	126	127	128	129	130	131	132		133	134	135	136	137	138	139	140	141	142
160	159	158	157	156	155	154	153		152	151	150	149	148	147	146	145	144	143
161	162	163	164	165	166	167	168		169	170	171	172	173	174	175	176	177	178
196	195	194	193	192	191	190	189		188	187	186	185	184	183	182	181	180	179
197	198	199	200	201	202	203	204		205	206	207	208	209	210	211	212	213	214
232	231	230	229	228	227	226	225		224	223	222	221	220	219	218	217	216	215
233	234	235	236	237	238	239	240		241	242	243	244	245	246	247	248	249	250
268	267	266	265	264	263	262	261		260	259	258	257	256	255	254	253	252	251
269	270	271	272	273	274	275	276		277	279	280	281	282	283	284	285	286	287
		303	302	301	300	299	298		297	296	295	294	293	292	291	290	289	288
		308	309	310	311	312	313		314	315	316	317	318	319	320	321	322	323
		339	338	337	336	335	334		333	332	331	330	329	328	327	326	325	324
			345	346	347	348	349		350	351	352	353	354	355	356	357	358	359
		374	373	372	371	370			369	368	367	366	365	364	363	362	361	360
		381	382	383	384	385			387	388	389	390	391	392	393	394	395	396
		411	410	409	408	407			406	405	404	403	402	401	400	399	398	397
		418	419	420	421	422			423	424	425	426	427	428	429	430	431	432
		447	446	445	444	443			442	441	440	439	438	437	436	435	434	433
		453	454	455	456	457			458	459	460	461	462	463	464	465	466	

To aid in locating graves, names from tombstones on the outside edge of the block are shown.

164

MAP 8:

BLOCK 5

Miller · Howard · Eaves · Anderson · Lucas · Carter · Ballard · Wilson

| | Pollard | Brown | Peal | Traylor | Harris | Traylor | Williams | Thomas | Coleman | Phillips | Prince | | Murdock | Marion | Morris | Huff | Hughes | | Watson | Crum |

EX 43 · EX 82 · EX 83 · EX 122 · EX 123

2 Ext · 41 Ext · 42 · 43 · 82 · 83 · 122 · 123 · 162 · 163

44 · 81 · 84 · 121 · 124 · 161

2 · 41 · 187 · 189 · Walker

3 · 40 · 45 · 80 · 85 · 120 · 125 · 160 · 186 · 190

4 · 39 · 46 · 79 · 86 · 119 · 126 · 159 · 185 · 191 · Turentine

5 · 38 · 47 · 78 · 87 · 118 · 127 · 158 · 184 · 192 · Reed

6 · 37 · 48 · 77 · 88 · 117 · 128 · 157 · 183 · 193 · Miller

7 · 36 · 49 · 76 · 89 · 116 · 129 · 156 · 182 · 194 · McPherson

8 · 35 · 50 · 75 · 90 · 115 · 130 · 155 · 181 · 195 · Marshall

9 · 34 · 51 · 74 · 91 · 114 · 131 · 154 · 180 · 196 · Matson

10 · 33 · 52 · 73 · 92 · 113 · 132 · 153 · 179 · 197 · Alexander

11 · 32 · 53 · 72 · 93 · 112 · 133 · 152 · 178 · 198 · Patterson

12 · 31 · 54 · 71 · 94 · 111 · 134 · 151 · 177 · 199 · Huff

13 · 30 · 55 · 70 · 95 · 110 · 135 · 150 · 176 · 200 · Johnson

14 · 29 · 56 · 69 · 96 · 109 · 136 · 149 · 175 · 201 · White

15 · 28 · 57 · 68 · 97 · 108 · 137 · 148 · 174 · 202 · Miller

16 · 27 · 58 · 67 · 98 · 107 · 138 · 147 · 173 · 203 · Perry

17 · 26 · 172 · 204 · Hill

18 · 25 · 59 · 66 · 99 · 106 · 139 · 146 · 164 · 171 · 205 · Stevens

19 · 24 · 60 · 65 · 100 · 105 · 140 · 145 · 165 · 170 · 206 · Little

20 · 23 · 61 · 64 · 101 · 104 · 141 · 144 · 166 · 169 · 207 · Jones

21 · 22 · 62 · 63 · 102 · 103 · 142 · 143 · 167 · 168 · 208 · Woodard

Crafton · Morris · Hood · Gipson · Fifer · Clay · Suttles · Maloney · Coe · Washington

To aid in locating graves, names from tombstones on the ouotside edge of the block are shown.

MAP 9:

EGGLESTON POST BLOCK (EP)

NORTH

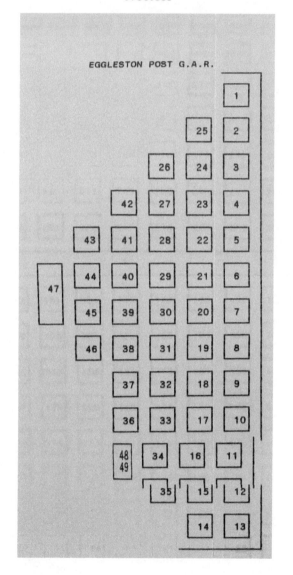

EGGLESTON POST G.A.R.

MAP 10:

POTTER'S FIELD (PF)

SOUTH

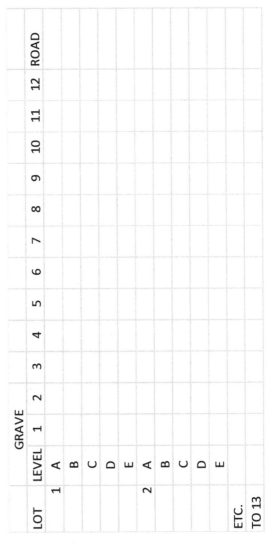

NORTH FENCE

MAP 11:

WICHITA (HIGHLAND) MAUSOLEUM

NORTH

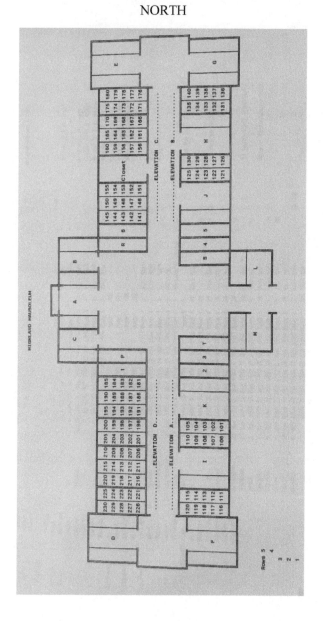

168

Bibliography

1922. *1922-23 Wichita Negro Yearbook.* Wichita: Negro Star Publishing.

1927. *1927-28 Wichita Negro Yearbook.* Wichita: Negro Star Publishing.

Advisory, Planning. 1950. "Cemeteries for the City Plan."

2011. *African American Resources in Wichita, Sedgwick County, KS 1870-1972.* NHRP submitted by Deon Wolfenbarger, approved by NPS approved June 28, 2011, Wichita: National Historic Register Preservation.

Baldwin, Sara Mullin. 1929. *Who's Who in Wichita, 1929.* Wichita: R. M. Baldwin Corp.

Beacon, Wichita. n.d.

Beacon, Wichita Eagle and. n.d.

Bentley, O H. 1910. *History of Wichita and Sedgwick County, Kansas, Past and Present, including an account of the cities, towns and villages of the county.* Wichita: C. F. Cooper and Co.

Bulletin, National Register. 2016. *Guidelines for Evaluating Registered Cemeteries and Burial Places.* November 7. Accessed November 7, 2016.

Campney, Brent M. S. 2015. *This is Not Dixie: Racist Violence in Kansas 1861-1927.* Urbana: Univeristy of Illinois Press.

Carter, D. W. 2013. *Mayday Over Wichita.* Charleston: The History Press.

Center, Touro Law. 2016. "The World of the Dead, The Right of Sepulcher, and the Power of Information." *Touro Law Review* Vol 32, No 4, Art 7: page 785-804.

Church, Episcopal. n.d. *A history of St. John's Episcopal Church in Wichita.* Wichita: Self published.

Clark, Dr. Howard C. n.d. *A History of the Sedgwick County Medical Society.* Wichita.

Commerce, Wichita Chamber of. 1946. *Wichita People.* Wichita: Wichita Chamber of Commerce.

Commission, Kansas Human Rights. 2006. "Letter regarding SB 2582." letter to update the KAAD and KADEA regulations of Covenants, Topeka.

Commission, Planning. 1937. "Form NS-8."

County, Sedgwick. n.d. *Sedgwick County Sheriff History.*

Courtwright, Julie. 2000. *Bits of Broken Dreams: The Life and Failure of Hanna Rea Woodman.* Masters' Thesis - School of History, Wichita: Wichita State University.

Crankshaw, Ned, et al. 2016. "The Lost Cause and Reunion in the Confederate Cemeteries of the North." *The Landscape Journal - University of Wisconsin.*

Cutler, William G. 1883. *History of the State of Kansas.* Chicago: A. T. Andreas.

DeArment, Robert K. 1979. *Bat Masterson. the Man and the Legend.* Norman: University of Oklahoma Press.

Directive 5120.36. 1963. (Secretary of State William McNamara).

Eagle, Wichita City. n.d.

Eagle, Wichita Daily. n.d.

Eick, Gretchen Cassel. 2001. *Dissent in Wichita-The Civil Rights Movement in the MIdwest, 1954-1972.* Urbana: University of Illinois.

Etcheson, Nicole. 2004. *Bleeding Kansas: Contested Liberty in the Civil War Era.* Lawrence: University Press of Kansas.

Executive Order 8802. 1941. (President Franklin D. Roosevelt).

Executive Order 9981. 1948. (President Harry S. Truman).

Farley, Ned Williams. 1998. *Maple Grove Cemetery 1900 to 1997: A Study of the Cemetery's Overal Demography and the Change in frequencies of One Hundred Randomly Sampled Surnames.".* Master's Thesis, Wichita: Wichita State University - Department of Anthropology.

Faust, Drew Gilpin. 2008. *This Republic of Suffering-Death and the American Civil War.* New York: Random House.

Fine-Dare, Kathleen S. 2002. *Grave Injustice: The American Indian Repatriation Movement and NAGPRA.* Lincoln: Univeristy of Nebraska Press.

Friend, Craig Thompson and Lorri Glover. 2015. *Death and the American South.* Cambridge: Cambridge University Press.

Gabrielson, Shirley, Don Granger, Carolyn Kell and Bill Sloan. 1994. *This is Who We Are: Archives of the Frist Presbyterian Church of Wichita.* Wichita: Self.

Gordon, LInda. 2017. *The Second Coming of the KKK-The Ku Klux Klan of the 1920s and the American Political Tradition.* New York: Liveright Publishing Co.

Greene, Meg. 2008. *Rest in Peace-A History of American Cemeteries.* Minneapolis: Twenty-First Century Books.

Groups, Institute of Cultures. 1970. *Institute of Cultures Exhibit, 1969-1970.* Wichita: Promotional brochure from the exhibit located at Century II.

n.d. *History of Chelsea, KS.*

Holloway, Karla F. C. 2002. *Passed On-African American Mourning Stories.* Durham: Duke University Press.

Hund-Milne, Susan and Marlene Smith-Graham. 1991. *A History of West Wichita: A collection of articles from Westside Story.* Wichita: Westside Story.

Irion, Paul E. 1964. *The Fuenral and the Mourners-Pastoral Care of the Bereaved.* Nashville: Abingdon Press.

Keister, Douglas. 2004. *Stories in Stone-A Field Guide to Cemetery Symbolism and Iconography.* Salt Lake City: Gibbs Smith, Publisher.

LePore, Jill. 2005. *New York Burning-Liberty, Slavery, and Conspiracy in Eighteenth-Century Manhattan.* New York: Random House.

Long, Dick. 1945. *Wichita 1866-1883.* Wichita: McCormick Armstrong.

—. 1969. *Wichita Century.* Wichita: Wichita Historical Museum Assn, Inc.

Marsh, Tanya D. Mar/Apr 2016. "When Dirt and Death Collide." *Probate & Property* Vol 30, Issue 2.

Marsha, Tanya. 2016. "When Dirt and Death Collide." *Probate and Property,* March/April: Vol 3, Issue 2.

Mason, James E. 2012. *Wichita*. Charleston: Arcadia Publishing.

—. 2011. *Wichita's Riverside Parks*. Charleston: Arcadia Publishing.

Mathewson, Richard J. n.d. *William Mathewson: The Original Buffalo Bill*.

McElya, Micki. 2016. *The Politics of Mourning-Death and Honor in Arlington National Cemetery*. Cambridge: Harvard University Press.

Mead, James R. 2008. *Hunting and Trading on the Great Plains, 1850-1875*. Wichita: Rowfant Press.

Miner, Craig. 2002. *Kansas: The History of the Sunflower State, 1854-2000*. Lawrence: University of Kansas Press.

—. 1982. *Wichita: The Early Years, 1865-1880*. Omaha: University of Nebraska Press.

—. 1988. *Wichita-The Magic City*. Wichita: Wichita-Sedgwick County Historical Museum.

Mitford, Jessica. 1998. *The American Way of Death*. New York: Alfred A Knopf, Inc.

Moeder, Rev. John M. 1937. *Early Catholicity in Kansas and History of the Diocese of Wichita*. Wichita: Diocesan Chancery Office.

Museum, The Kansas African American. 2015. *African Americans of Wichita*. Charleston: Arcadia Publishing.

Operations, Sedgwick County Division of Information. 2006. "Basic Genealogical Research Resources." April 2017.

Painter, Nell Irvin. 1992. *Exodusters: African American Migration to Kansas After Reconstruction*. New York: W. W. Norton & Co.

Patterson, Andrea. 2008. "Germs and Jim Crow." *Journal of the History of Biology*, Spring.

Pratt, George B. 1889. *The Magic City - Wichita*. Neenah: Art Publishing Co.

Price, Jay and Keith Wondra. 2013. *Wichita: 1930-2000*. Charleston: Arcadia Publishing.

Price, Jay. 2003. *Wichita: 1860-1930*. Charleston: Arcadia Publishing.

Rhoads, Loren. 2017. *199 Cemeteries To See Before You Die*. New York: Black Dog & Leventhal Publishers.

Rights, Commission on Civil. 1977. "School Desegregation in Wichita."

Rives, Bob. 2004. *Baseball in Wichita*. Charleston : Arcadia Publishing.

Rosa, Joseph G and Waldo K Koop. 1989. *Rowdy Joe Lowe: Gambler with a Gun*. Norman: University of Oklahoma Press.

Rothstein, Richard. 2017. *The Color of Law-A Forgotten History of How our Government Segregated America*. New York: Liveright Publishing Co.

Russell, Dick. 2009. *African American Genius: Inspirational Portraits of African American Leaders*. New York: Skyhouse Publishing.

Russell, John Caro Jr and Walter Broadnax. 1968. *Minorities in Kansas: A Quest for Equal Opportunity*. Topeka: Office of the Governor Economic Opportunity Office.

Rutledge, Carol Brunner. 1979. *The Story of Wichita*. Wichita: Wichita Public Schools.

Sayer, Duncan. 2010. *Ethics and Burial Archaeology*. London: Duckworth.

Scarre, Chris and Geoffrey Scarre. 2006. *The Ethics of Archaeology*. New York: Cambridge University.

Sloan, Charles William Jr. 1970. *The Leagl Ouster of the Ku Klux Klan From Kansas, 1922-1927*. Master's Thesis, Wichita: Wichita State Univeristy - Department of History.

Smith, Suzanne E. 2010. *To Serve the Living-Funeral Directors and the African American Way of Death*. Cambridge: Belknap Press of Harvard University Press.

Tanner, Beccy. 1991. *Bear Grease, Builders and Bandits*. Wichita: Wichita Eagle and Beacon Publishing Co.

2015. *The World of the Dead, The Right of Sepulcher and the Power of Information*. Cour of Appeals, Shipley V City of NY, New York: Tuoro Law Review.

Van Meter, Sondra. 1977. *Our Common School Heritage*. Shawnee mission: Inter-Collegiate Press.

Wessler, Seth Freed. 2015. "Black Deaths Matter." *The Nationa*, November 2.

Wichita City Ordinance #325. 1906.

Wondra, Keith and Barb Myers. 2016. *Old Cowtown Museum*. Charleston: Arcadia Publishing.

Wondra, Keith. 2014. *Where the Old West Comes to Life: The Story of Old Cowtown Museum*. Master's Thesis, Wichita: Wichita State University - Department of HIstory.

Wood, L. Curtise. 1969. *Dynamics of Faith: Wichita People*. Wichita: Wichita State University, College of Business.

Woodman, Hannah Rea. 1948. *Wichitana 1877-1897*. Wichita: Wichita Sedgwick County Historical Museum.

Yalom, Marilyn. 2008. *The American Resting Place-Four Hundred Years of History Through our Cemeteries and Burial Grounds*. Boston: Houghton Mifflin Co.

Yearout, Joshua L. 2010. *Wichita Jazz and Vice Between the World Wars*. Wichita: Rowfant Press.

Zoning Codes. 2015. Wichita City Ordinance 2015-05-033

Zoning Codes. 2015. Sedgwick County Resolution 136-2015

CERTAIN WEBSITES ACCESSED:

Department of Interior – Bureau of Land Management, Eastern States

    www.blm.gov

City of Wichita – Park Department

    Wichita.gov/parkandrec/cityparks/pages/cemeteries.aspx

Find A Grave

    FindAGrave.com

Kansas Genealogy Trails

    Genealogytrails.com

Ks Gen Web – Sedgwick County Genealogical Research

    KsGenWeb.org/Sedgwick/cems/highcem.html

Midwest Historical Genealogical Society

    MHGSwichita.org

Sedgwick County Register of Deeds – for plats and tax records

    SedgwickCounty.org

    GIS.Sedgwick.gov

INDEX:

I

W

XYZ